PIAZZA DI SPAGNA
TRINITÀ DEI MONTI
PINCIO

Pastasciutta in Bianco
Fegatelli
Pizza Napoletana

Pasta Ceci
all' Umido
Frascati

COLOSSEUM
PIAZZA VENEZIA

Zuppa di Pesce

nana
telli

ROMAN FORUM
THE PALATINE
ARCH OF CONSTANTINE
VIA APPIA ANTICA
TOMB OF
CÆCILIA METELLA   CATACOMBS

Pollo alla Diavola
Pizza coi Funghi

Fritti
Fettuccine Sugo e Burro
Abbacchio al
Forno
St. Honoré Red wine of Olevano

GIANICOLO   TRASTEVERE

Pastasciutta alla Poverella
Involtini
Insalata
Mozzarella in
Carozza

naretti
go
selli
lese

VENUS
OF THE
CAPITOL

THE DYING GAUL
MARCUS AURELIUS

Spaghetti con
Aglio-Olio-Peperoncino Stufato
WALK TO CAMPO DI FIORI

Calzone

THE FINE ART OF ROMAN COOKING

Also by Alexander Lenard

WINNIE ILLE PU
A Latin Version of A. A. Milne's *Winnie-the-Pooh*

THE VALLEY OF THE LATIN BEAR

The Fine Art of
ROMAN
COOKING

by Alexander Lenard

TRANSLATED BY ELISABETH ABBOTT

Illustrations by Eva Hohrath

E. P. Dutton & Co., Inc.   New York   1966

CONTENTS

THE FINE ART OF ROMAN COOKING

PREFACE AND DIRECTIONS FOR THIS AND ALL OTHER COOKBOOKS, OR THE FARMER'S WIFE IN THE CASTLE

Whenever guests were entertained at the castle, the poor farmer's wife was summoned to help the cook, himself an important man in his own right. There she split wood, peeled potatoes, cleaned chickens, stirred the cake—and then went home and told her husband all about it.

"Oh! What a feast that was! What a dinner! And at the end there was a strawberry custard cream cake so good it made the lords' and ladies' mouths water!"

Each time the farmer listened silently to this tale—until one day he lost his patience, banged on the table, and shouted: "All right! Now I'm going to have a strawberry cream cake too!"

"But we haven't any strawberries!" said the farmer's wife.

"We've got plenty of dried pears. Make it with pears!"

"Yes, but we haven't any butter for the filling!"

"Make it with lard."

"But where can I get that beautiful white flour? We have only half a bag of rye."

"Rye isn't bad. Make it with rye."

"And what about the eggs? The dozen eggs?"

"By thunder! Can't a man ever get the better of you women? I told you I wanted that cake. Now go to the kitchen and make it!"

The woman went to the kitchen; she sifted, stirred, baked, waited . . . and came back with the cake, still without a word. The farmer was not inclined to talk either. He cut a piece of the cake, took a bite and ate it.

"You see!" he exclaimed. Then he added slowly: "But I can't understand why it made the lords' and ladies' mouths water."

ʊ̈ʊ̈ FIRST
YOU TAKE...

a history book . . . I beg your pardon. . . . We want to go to the kitchen. But the kitchen is in Rome. When you come out of the station in Rome, you face a section of the old city wall that has confronted travelers to the Eternal City for two thousand years. When you arrive by jet plane, you fly over the granaries and theaters of Ostia Antica, which are every bit as old as the wall. The traveler who comes from the north by auto drives over the Ponte Milvio, on which the soldiers of the Emperor Maxentius fought when IN HOC SIGNE VINCES appeared in the sky, the same bridge over which Goethe's coach rumbled on its way to Rome. When you approach the city from the south, you pass along the Via Appia, which at the time of the above-mentioned battle also had more than five hundred years behind it.

It makes no difference how you come to the city, to the hearth, to Vesta's holy of holies, the way always leads past thousands of years. In the old palaces between the Tiber and the Piazza Navona, charcoal fires still glow and their smoke blackens the walls of the *atrium*. The matron who presides at the hearth still rules over the entire family that is gathered

around her. The choicest dishes are still prepared in earthen pots and pans; and in Rome, the preparation of a cabbage soup is the continuation of an historical ritual.

This does not mean that we have anything against modern kitchens, gas, electricity, metal pots and pans. We cooks of today have an easier time, but the gastronome will have none of these modern inventions. The *erudita et docta palata* (the subtle and sophisticated palates), the *magister cenandi* (the gourmet) continue, now as before, to insist upon having the classic dishes cooked over the steady flame of the charcoal stove and served in the warmth of earthenware dishes. True, the charcoal stove smokes a little. And carrying coals is sometimes tiring—it also blackens your hands. But to the connoisseur, the magic utensil has the unprecedented advantage of compelling the cook to stand in front of it and fan the fire. Her attention is therefore centered on her work. *La sventola* (the fan) is the symbol of power over cookery. The first thing the pupil of the culinary art in Rome must learn is the correct way to fan the fire. After five minutes the beginner thinks her hand will break in two. But little girls of ten fan the fire under the beanpot three hours at a time without getting tired. It is like playing the piano: ten minutes of Czerny exhausts one, but *The Well-Tempered Clavichord* rests the hand.

Fire is a living thing. Watching the fire, one is never bored.

Time does not drag for the Roman housewife who fans the fire. She does not find the hours at the stove wasted as do other women who turn on the electric current and stand there with nothing to do. And if she can fan from her wrist alone, the rhythm of the gently swaying feather helps her to ponder her responsibilities as head of the household.

He who tries to deprive the Roman matron of her charcoal stove and fan draws down upon his head the wrath of Vesta: his Tiber eels with peas will never have the flavor that moved emperors and popes to pious thoughts. *Dura lex sed lex.* . . . Hard as Rome's laws were, they had to be obeyed, and they are valid *per omnia saecula saeculorum.* Roasts should be cooked over a charcoal fire, stuffed tomatoes in an earthen pan, calf's stomach in an iron kettle, and lamb as well as bread belong in the oven.

Even those reformers who are always trying to change the structure of society must admit that they cannot improve on a culinary recipe. How much has happened in Rome since the first laurel-crowned priest of Apollo looked upon the liver of the sacrificial animal and took it home with him for his noonday meal!

Marcus Gavius Apicius who, in the days of Tiberius, wrote the only Roman cookbook that has come down to us (let us lay aside the feather fan and make his spirit a smoke-offering), tells us how from time immemorial—or at least *ab urbe condita,* from the founding of the city—liver was cooked.

Cut pieces of liver into strips about as long as your thumb but twice as thick, cover them with bay leaves, wrap them in a piece of the caul (omentum) of the sacrificial animal, and roast them on a grill or a spit over the open fire.

And today anyone who orders *fegatelli* in a *trattoria,* or restaurant of the less pretentious sort, where they roast and grill according to the old traditions, will find Apicius' dish again, and with it he will receive a lesson in antiquity that his palate will not soon forget. He will understand why the Deipnosophistai, Athenaeus' well-fed philosophers who, in 118 A.D., argued over food, drink and theater, tested this dish carefully and even debated whether the Greek word for caul should be pronounced *"epiplon"* or *"epiploon."*

Had it not been for Apicius, it would not have been easy for Roman cookery to show convincing proof of its noble antiquity. It seems almost a miracle that this invaluable document has been preserved for us. In the centuries of turmoil and chaos, almost all knowledge of cookery that had been gathered over a thousand years was lost.

But not quite all. For before the last upheaval men of culture fled with their possessions to the periphery of other cultured societies; and in this way costly manuscripts from Rome wandered to Ireland and to the Spanish borders, where the works of our once famous, though later forgotten and unsung, Apicius were preserved.

Ancient authors mention three gourmets by the name of Apicius, which proves that the family kept up the best culinary traditions. A later descendant of the family sent a gift of marinated oysters from Rome to the Emperor Trajan on the battlefield, and Athenaeus assures us that they arrived fresh and in perfect condition. Pliny called the great Apicius *altissimus gurges* (sublime gullet); Juvenal spoke of him as *exemplum gulae* (example of a gourmand); and the Church Father Tertullian referred to him as "the discoverer of excellent sauces." Seneca relates that Apicius squandered a hundred million sesterces. When he went over his accounts and found he had only ten million left, he took poison to avoid dying of hunger. He "was a champion of gastronomy and through his teachings he corrupted his era"—*disciplina sua saeculum infecit.* The philosopher is obviously harsh and unjust. If a man squandered millions, especially in peacetime when girls at the Colosseum gave strangers a smile for three obols, he must have entertained his friends constantly and on the most lavish scale. Could he have forgotten the philosophers? Shouldn't we rather translate the passage to mean "he aroused his century's enthusiasm for his art"?

For two things, however, he was never denied credit: he discovered that if geese were fed dried sweet figs they would have a beautiful soft liver. (*Ficatum* this was called in those days, from which we have the Italian *fegato*, liver.) And he wrote a cookbook so that no one should be deprived of the pleasures of his table.

"A statue outlives a city, a verse outlasts a bronze," a poet once wrote. But what about a cookbook? "In a literary work, whether poetry, oration or educational articles, the form of the presentation will be noticed and faithfully preserved with its contents, whereas the form of a cookbook is unimportant and the contents, on which alone it depends, will be made to fit the changing needs of the times and be further developed," says Edward Brandt, the famous Apicius expert, in speaking of the fate of the "X libri," the "Ten Books." Times changed; new editors dedicated new recipes to new emperors—even Julian the Apostate was given a brain sauce to accompany semolina pudding, although he was as ill-disposed toward the culinary art as to Christianity (he fired his court cooks). A literary reviser translated from the Greek certain recipes for cold desserts, a fecula pudding and cold mulled wine (old Falernian wine and young Hymettus honey mixed). Methods of preserving foods were copied, and in the year 400 A.D. a physician added diet recipes in Vulgar Latin. In those days, however, Africa had long since ceased to export any resinous *laserpicium;* pepper (which even in Trimalchius' day was so expensive that his wife ground it herself, in a mill made of boxwood), had disappeared, and stewed dormice were crossed off the bill of fare. Apicius' book was out of date.

For long, long years it lay in the libraries of monasteries where monks made worm-eaten copies in Carolingian or Anglo-Saxon script. Philosophers in the Middle Ages were interested in the soul, but not in the thing that holds body and soul together. It is worth mentioning, however, that during the Dark Ages nearly all the manuscripts belonging to that fattener of geese (who also gave instructions for preserving truffles) remained in France, a circumstance which is not to be overlooked when the origin of truffled Strasbourg goose-liver pâté is discussed.

Five hundred years had passed since the last copy of Apicius' book was made, when Latinists opened the doors of the monasteries' libraries and let in a breath of fresh air. The humanist Poggio Bracciolini came to Fulda and made a note of what was to be found there. "Eight books by Apicius," he wrote in his haste—he was not collecting cookbooks, you see, but anecdotes, which he published at the end of his life. However his catalogue fell into the hands of the learned Pope Nicolas V, founder of the Vatican library, who commissioned the Medicis' tutor, Enoch of Ascoli, to bring him the valuable manuscript.

Enoch hastened to Fulda and, while there, he also visited the Scandinavian libraries. When, five years later, he returned with his rich booty, Nicolas had died and his successor, Calixtus III, was perfectly satisfied with the papal cuisine. He refused to purchase the manuscript. The unfortunate discoverer then set out in search of a culture-minded prince, but death overtook him. His schoolmate, Aeneas Silvius Piccolomini, came to the funeral, took away Tacitus' *Germania*, but was not interested in sauces because he was just then writing that charming love story of Euryalus and Lucretia. Apicius' manuscript then disappeared again for a few more decades.

Whether because Cardinal Bressarion arranged for something new, or because industrious Florentine clerks produced beautiful copies of everything they could lay their hands on, in the year 1498 the first printed edition appeared in Milan. *Apicius culinarius* was the title of the first edition; *De re coquinaria*, "concerning cooking," was added to the second edition. The book was immediately pirated in Venice. Somewhat later, on the island of Megalona near Montpellier, the physician Albanus Torinus found a badly mutilated Codex which he published in Basel in 1541, and a year later his colleague, Gabriel Humelberg, who possessed better copies, added *De obsoniis et condimentis* (Concerning Garnishes and Condiments) on the title page.

Physicians were therefore responsible for rediscovering Apicius, for as they both say in their foreword, "Dietetics is a branch of medicine." Professional humanists were less enthusiastic: "What sort of Latin is this," they asked, "in which there is talk of juices like *garum, oxygarum,* and *hydrogarum,* and of things that are found neither in Caesar's nor in Cicero's works? What do *mammotestus, siccoparsum* and *leucozomus* mean?" "Kitchen Latin!" cried Kaspar Barthius scornfully—obviously he had no appetite. *Verba semibarbara!* Take the book away!"

One hundred and fifty years later another physician, Martin Lister, physician in ordinary to Queen Anne of England, made a timid attempt to publish Apicius again. The little book appeared in only one hundred and fifty copies and was pirated in Holland in 1709. Then followed another one hundred and fifty years of silence.

Around the year 1850, after scholars had sufficiently exhausted all the classical authors, many of them turned their attention again to the old gourmand, but this time only to destroy him completely. Everyone knows you can't make up cookbooks out of whole cloth any more than you can epic poems. Just as it was possible to prove that Homer had never lived, so too in later years doubt was cast on the existence of Apicius—a doubt still found today in many great encyclopedias.

A later age brought about a change. Serious debates began with the critical edition of 1922. In the domain of sauces, in which the most essential method of archaeology—excavation—failed, classical philology had to come to the rescue. After his recipes had been arranged in sections including measures and seasonings, and in other sections describing simple methods of cooking, and after discarding the thermospodion group (those in favor of using hot ashes instead of wood or coal stoves), the tractogalactis group (cooking with pasta and milk), and finally the salsacaccabia directions (for salt dishes cooked in a pot), Apicius' real recipes were left. The fish dumplings (*isacia marina*) recommended by Emperor Heliogabalus were probably added later. Edward Brandt, whose clever research earned him his doctor's degree, blames Marcus Gavius Apicius for only one thing: that the one hundred and thirty-eight sauce recipes "make a frivolous impression." But here the historian of cookery must firmly contradict his philological colleague: if the Italian of today serves his *pastasciutta* with just as many sauces, he does so not only for variety but in order to eat as cheaply as possible. The old Romans by no means lived on bread and circus games alone, as one sometimes thinks; they insisted upon having a different *embractum* or *impensa* every day in which to dip their bread.

When it comes to seasoned sauces, purely scientific methods have their natural limits. To continue the Apician work is reserved only for cooks, and though our classical education is so deficient that for the verb "to eat" we sometimes say *comedere*, sometimes *manducare*, nevertheless we know better than all the Latin professors that we must have everything at our fingertips, and just exactly how much rosemary and bay leaf the roast pork must have if it is to taste as it did when the *epulones*, the priests in charge of the sacrificial banquets, wolfed it down in Jupiter's Temple on the Capitol to amuse the god and keep him in a good humor.

Traditions are said to be particularly long-lived on islands. On the Tiber island in Rome where the Temple of Aesculapius stood, hospitalers are still active today. But Rome itself, behind its girdle of walls, was also a sort of island. Its ability not only to make history but to preserve it, to maintain a certain mood for thousands of years, is unparalleled; Rome remained true to itself even when (like all of us) it had to recast the past a little. All Saints' Day was celebrated for the first time in the Pantheon, the temple of all gods. But liver continued to be cooked as it was in the days of Apollo. Michelangelo piled the Pantheon up on the roof of St. Peter's . . . but worthy Roman matrons continued to fan the fire of Vesta *all'ombra del Cupolone* (in the shadow of the great cupola). Catastrophes befell the city; mercenaries sacked it, guns thundered on the Castel Sant'Angelo, fire leaped to the roofs of houses . . . and was forced back under the cooking pot. A hundred years ago guns roared at the Porta Pia and again strangers appeared at the gates: the Red Shirts.

"Rome is the capital of Italy," one learns in school. In a certain sense that is true. But it is also true that the Romans had no desire to nudge Florence out of her role as Italy's leading city, a title which, as the home of Dante and of the beautiful Tuscan tongue, belonged to her by rights. To be sure, the pontifical government was fairly conservative, and while in other parts of Italy railroads (which Pope Pius IX branded as an invention of the devil) were being built, the executioner hired by the Papal States, Maestro Titta, was still quartering poor wretches on the Piazza del Popolo—though out of respect for the humanitarian tendencies of the century he had the poor fellows knocked out first with a club. However, a bad government that levies no taxes is always better than one that takes money from you; and to the Roman rice-eating Lombardians, polenta-eating Venetians, and Sicilians, who speak an incomprehensible language, were all equally foreign.

The Red Shirts marched on Rome with the best intentions . . . but they opened the way for the more dangerous Black Shirts. The papal cannon of the year 1871 would have driven off that bunch of Catilinian revolutionaries, but in 1921 the cannon were in the Museum, and through the old breach marched a paunchy, bald-headed journalist whose outthrust underjaw gave a false impression of strength. "Marched" is perhaps somewhat exaggerated, because for safety's sake he had come on the railroad—which may be a devilish invention after all.

With his arrival the destruction of the city began. Entire sections were razed in order to open avenues for parades. The ancient houses on the slope of the Capitol, the *borghi* between St. Peter's and the Tiber, with their old kitchens, old hearths, disappeared. A film city, Cinecittà, was built in order to give a false impression of the rest. . . . Before his flight (he was a coward, which was the difference between him and Catiline) the dictator drove oil and flour out of the pantries, and to make up for it, had cabbages planted in the public gardens. When they spoke of the *"foro Mussolini,"* people referred not to his white marble forum, but to the last hole (*foro*) in their belts.

His downfall left behind a deplorable Rome. Without the old streets, without the walls from the Middle Ages, without the quiet, secluded courtyards, the city stood open to culinary barbarians. They brought their own food with them, pre-cooked food in cans, needing only to be spooned out. Savages came who cooked spaghetti in its own juices, cut it with knives, and ate it with a spoon. A drink that Scots in far off Scotland brewed in smoky malt kilns was poured down at meals to the ruin of the taste buds. The foreigners ate something they called "hot dogs. . . ."

That it is nevertheless still possible today to order a fragrant *abbacchio*—a crisply roasted baby lamb—is due to the fact that the Roman culinary calendar is as firmly entrenched in the minds and reflexes of every Roman as the church calendar itself. To the great events in the universe ("if in limitless space the identical repeats itself and flows eternally," as Goethe, a well-known admirer of Roman cookery, said) this culinary calendar reacts rhythmically within its own microcosm.

Every New Year enters the city with pig's feet—to be more precise, with pig's feet from Modena or Cremona, the city which is most unjustly known only for old violins. Lentils accompany the "little trotters," for everyone knows they mean money, ready cash. January 6, Epiphany—or as they say in Italy *Befana*—is the day of all sorts of sweetmeats, which are displayed on the Piazza Navona; the 16th is the day of

holy Bishop Honorius, after whom a marvelous cake is named. The 19th day of March, on the other hand, belongs in the church calendar to St. Joseph, in the culinary calendar to *bignès* (fritters), light, hollow puff pastries sprinkled with white vanilla sugar, that bob gracefully on the fat in the pan. Easter week soon follows with lamb and beef soup; the *pizze pasquale*, Easter pastries; and the lamb roast which emerges from the dark oven in an aroma of garlic and rosemary. Soon artichokes and peas take over, and nowhere are they so tender, so beautifully green as on Roman plates. There is a long-established affinity between Tiber eels and peas, between ham from Parma and peas, between young squid and peas, and fortunate is the traveler who has tasted these combinations! Strawberries from Nemi, cherries from Arezzo mean May and June; yellow melons and watermelons herald the approach of summer, whose highpoint is the great feast of snails on San Giovanni's Day, the solstice. The old Romans ate snails at funeral meals; the new Romans eat

them when the sun begins to set and wash them down with
wine to fan the glow a little longer. Fall brings peaches that
come to Rome from Castel Gandolfo at the same time as the
Holy Father. Their flesh is deep gold, their fragrance delicious. Pour cognac over them, cover them with vanilla ice
cream, top it all with whipped cream and you have not
wasted these noble ingredients. Soon shepherds come bring-
ing their gifts too—*ricotta* cheese makes an excellent filling
for *cannelloni* or pasta squares; dredged with sugar and rum
it appears at the end of the Sunday midday meal; and between these two extremes lies a wide variety of choice:
ricotta with onions and pepper, *ricotta* with cinnamon and
sugar, *ricotta* with coffee . . . there are endless ways in which
to prepare it.

The end of autumn brings broccoli, that green plant not
unlike cauliflower. Broccoli and pasta with the neck and ribs
of the little black pigs from the Abruzzi make a soup the
memory of which lures even the Roman living abroad back
to his native land again.

On All Souls' Day (The Day of the Dead) appear the
fave dei morti (beans of the dead), an old and tragic name
for an almond pastry, but it helps to lighten the mood of
sorrow. Roasted chestnuts usher in the season of the Saturnalia, the merry holiday mood in which even slaves were
allowed to speak as free men—or, as we say today, the Merry
Christmas season. . . .

The microcosm of the culinary week is enclosed in the
macrocosm of the culinary year. Guests in great hotels do
not notice this, however, for those materialistic institutions
no longer follow the rhythm that governs the mysterious cycle
of the seasons. But cooks and guests of the truly Roman cult
of gastronomy know better. Stroll into one of the *trattorie*
on the Piazza Navona or in the neighborhood of the Pantheon
and you will find that Jupiter is still powerful enough to

overthrow the dominion of pasta for one day in the week—
Giovedi (Thursday). On that day the bill of fare offers
potato noodles (*gnocchi*) with *ragù* (stew) or, on especially
festive occasions, with melted butter and Parmesan cheese—
a dish fully worthy of the thunder-hurling Olympian. Friday
brings the penitent return to Christianity—the inevitable dried
salt cod which was soaked under running water the evening
before. Its odor spares the initiate a glance at the calendar!
Chick-peas with rosemary to begin the meal, and codfish
at the end of the meal are served on fifty-two Fridays in
the year. Saturdays, on the other hand, bring a special experience: *trippa alla romana,* tripe in tomato sauce with
Parmesan cheese, to which a mint leaf is added. Real Romans
—the *"romani de Roma"*—do not eat at home on Saturdays
but flock to the places where *trippa* is prepared in great iron
pots. Sunday finds them at home again enjoying homemade
egg noodles—*fettuccine fatte in casa*—an excellent way to
praise the Lord's day.

And this routine never varies. Dictators may come and
dictators may go, but the tripe goes on cooking in the same
kettle; gods may fall, believers and skeptics may quarrel, but
all agree that the Capitoline Jupiter deserves his *gnocchi*
(potato noodles) and that Divine Providence and the Nor-
wegians discovered the codfish to make Friday (which always belongs a little to Venus and is called *Venerdi*) a
pleasanter day.

Before us chaos still lies. Only prophets are granted the
privilege of foreseeing the future. As to the future of Roman
cookery, St. Malachy warns us not to trust to the perma-
nence of earthly arrangements. His prophecy, said to have
been written in the year 1139, but certainly printed in 1595,
names as future popes Pope Pius XI (*fides intrepida*—stead-
fast faith); Pius XII (*pastor angelicus,* the diplomat pope,
the ambassador, the *nuntius*); John XXIII (*pastor et nauta,*

pope and sailor: he carried the Holy of Holies in the gondola in Venice); Paul VI (*flos florum,* the flower of flowers; his coat of arms as a cardinal was the lily). Still to come are *de medietate lunae* (he of the middle of the moon), *de labore solis* (he of the eclipse of the sun), *de gloria olivae* (the glory of the olive) . . . and "in the time of the final persecution of the Church, a Petrus Romanus will lead his flock in much adversity, after which the City on the Seven Hills will be destroyed and a terrible judge will judge the people."

Four more popes. . . . Even if the saint has prophesied correctly, it is worthwhile to collect the recipes of Roman cookery, to follow them carefully, to enjoy the result quietly, and to accompany them with a noble wine.

Nec Babylonios temptaris numeros . . . "Give up the astrologer's art," Horace advises us. *Carpe diem, quam minimum credula postero.* . . . Enjoy today and have no fear for the morrow.

೪೪ FRITTI
Fried Foods

Cities have souls, their own distinctive odors. London
smells of malt, Copenhagen of the sea and herring, and the
old, narrow streets of Rome have their own special smell.
In many places this odor is mixed with the fragrance from
boiling pots. . . . The stroller will more readily venture into
the shops of the *friggitori* (vendors of fried foods) than the
taverns; he need only point to the food that tempts him and
he gets it at once without a word. And the epicure gladly
follows him, for he knows that you can eat cheaper and
better there than anywhere else. He also knows how difficult
it is to make the *fritti* at home; they are best when swimming
in a sea of fat in an iron pot, to be fished out by the expert
at exactly the right moment.

From a culinary standpoint, Italy could be divided into
three provinces: the butter section coinciding with the Alpine
foreland, the oil section comprising Tuscany and Etruria, and
the South, which uses pork fat.

Roman *friggitori* are not dogmatic. They use olive oil for
fish and lard for all other *fritti*, though they have no objection to combining lard and oil, which has the advantage of

26

not sputtering and foaming as much as other fats. Suet, particularly the fat skimmed off the top of cold meat soups, may also be used to fry the *fritti* when they are to be eaten at once and piping hot. But take care you don't burn your tongue! You must first cool the *fritti* by squeezing several drops of lemon on them. Serve them with lemon wedges.

SUPPLÌ
Rice Patties (or Rice Rolls)

Rice was brought to Rome fairly late and was received with a certain amount of mistrust. It was known as the food of the Milanese, who make a truly excellent golden *risotto* with butter, marrow, and saffron. Milan and Rome have always looked askance at one another. The Milanese cannot forgive the Romans because the "Urbs" has not put up many factories, except for making stamps, and yet lives happily. The Romans take it ill of the Milanese because they speak a language impossible to understand, because they let themselves be overcharged for everything they buy, whether medicine or Christmas cakes, and because they are so like the Swiss. That in spite of this Rome uses rice in its *supplì* is proof of its cosmopolitan spirit.

1 small onion, chopped	1 teaspoon salt
3 tablespoons butter	1 teaspoon black pepper
1 cup rice (preferably Italian)	2 eggs, well beaten
2 cups meat juices (page 102– 104) or broth	½ cup grated Parmesan cheese
	Fat for frying

Sauté onion in butter in heavy saucepan. Add rice. When hot gradually add meat juices or broth, stirring constantly. Cover and cook 10 minutes, then add salt, and continue cooking for 15 minutes or until rice is tender. By this time it may be necessary to add a little more liquid. Off the stove mix in the pepper, eggs, and Parmesan cheese. Set aside to cool. Out of this mixture, and without adding anything, thrifty housewives can make *supplì* (or little croquettes) about as long as your thumb and two thumbs thick. Roll them in bread crumbs and fry in hot fat until golden brown. Serves 4 to 6.

True gastronomes prefer to fill the *supplì* first. The simplest filling is cheese—a small stick or slice of Mozzarella cheese which, when the *supplì* are hot, pulls into long threads when you bite off a piece. In Rome *provatura* was formerly used; today they use Mozzarella, a cheese made from buffalo milk. (In America, Mozzarella may be purchased in many supermarkets and any Italian grocery.) An unknown poet once compared these cheese threads to telephone wires, and since then these cheese *supplì* have been known as *supplì al telefono*.

It is more trouble (and more pleasure) to make *supplì al ragù*. In this *ragù* (ragout or stew) we use chicken livers and hearts, onions and tomatoes. Chop 2 chicken livers and hearts, 1 onion and 1 tomato, and sauté them quickly in 1 tablespoon fat, then pour meat juices (see pages 102–104) or broth over them and cook till tender and fairly dry. A tablespoon of the ragout is then placed on the rice *supplì*, which is rolled around the filling to form a croquette.

There are no objections to using both fillings. The connoisseur gives the highest award to the cheese-ragout combination, called *Supplì come Dio comanda* (as God commands). We must also point out that the same God orders the *supplì* to be eaten just hot enough not to burn your tongue.

CARCIOFI FRITTI
Fried Artichokes

The artichoke is a thistle from the Abyssinian highland. It first appeared in Rome around the seventeenth century and has since conquered vast stretches of the surrounding country. With peas it shares the reputation of growing better in the Latium region than in any other part of Italy. Roman artichokes are round and tender; the finest are called *cimaroli*. During Lent they are the favorite dish on every table in the city.

We cookbook writers cannot give our readers the ability to distinguish between young and old artichokes. There is, however, a difference in the way to prepare young artichokes and old artichokes, and in this case we shall make an exception and let youth take precedence.

8 young artichokes	All-purpose flour
Juice of 1 lemon	2 eggs, well beaten
1 teaspoon salt	Oil for deep frying
1/8 teaspoon pepper	Lemon wedges
2 tablespoons olive oil	

Cut the stem, leaving about 1 inch. Remove the hard outer leaves of the noble thistle. Peel off the outer skin of the stem, and cut off the tough points of the leaves with scissors. Then, depending upon its size, cut the artichoke into 6-10 pieces (or into quarters). Remove chokes and lay the pieces in a shallow dish containing the lemon juice, water to cover, salt, pepper, and olive oil. Lemon juice helps preserve the beautiful green color. Let stand 10 minutes. Drain and dry artichoke pieces.

Heat the oil for deep frying in the saucepan until it is moderately hot, dip the artichoke pieces in flour, then in egg, and fry in the hot oil till crisp and golden. Fry only a few at a time as too many at once will cool the oil. Serves 4.

Older artichokes, and those that come from a distance, must

first be parboiled for 10-15 minutes before being placed in lemon juice and oil (as above). Dry them, roll them in flour, and fry in moderately hot oil. Serve them with lemon wedges.

CERVELLI E ANIMELLE FRITTI
Fried Brains and Sweetbreads

Sheep and lambs' brains are best adapted to deep frying. The brains and sweetbreads of calf may also be used.

1½ pounds brains and sweetbreads of sheep, lamb, or calf
2 tablespoons vinegar
Juice of 1 lemon
¾ teaspoon salt
⅛ teaspoon pepper
2 sprigs parsley
All-purpose flour
1 egg, well beaten
Olive oil
Lemon wedges

First remove the membrane from the brain and wash well in cold water to get rid of the blood. With sweetbreads it is sufficient to remove the strings and connective tissues. Put brains and sweetbreads in cold water to cover, and add vinegar. Bring to a boil.

As soon as the water boils, remove the brains and sweetbreads, cut them in 2-inch pieces, and let them rest in a marinade of lemon juice, salt, pepper, and parsley for a quarter of an hour or, better, for half an hour. When ½ inch oil is bubbling briskly in the skillet, roll the pieces in flour, dip into egg, fry them for about 10 minutes in hot oil, turning once. Serves 4.

Repetitio est mater studiorum, said the old Romans. Repetition is an aid to learning. We therefore repeat: do not forget the lemon wedges.

FEGATO DI VITELLO FRITTO
Fried Calf's Liver

Calf (or sheep) liver (about 1½
   pounds)
All-purpose flour
1¼ teaspoons salt

¼ teaspoon pepper
1 egg, well beaten
2 tablespoons olive oil

Cut the calf or sheep's liver in finger-length slices (or about 4 inches long by 1½ inches thick). Roll in flour that has been mixed with salt and pepper, and then in egg. Sauté them for only 2 minutes in the hot oil. The liver may be added to a *fritto misto* (mixed fry) to give it more variety. Serves 4.

PAN DORATO
"Gilded Bread"

Artichokes, brains, sweetbreads, and liver, accompanied by white bread or a *panino* (roll), make a *fritto* that serves as an excellent midday meal, especially with a glass of Frascati (or any good dry white wine) to quench one's thirst. The traveler who has spent the forenoon trudging around museums and churches will gladly devote a moment at noon to the culinary art—and sit down to a *fritto* with *pan dorato* in a simple *rosticceria. Pan dorato* is an excellent addition to the *fritti.*

Italian white bread
4 eggs, well beaten
Meat broth or gravy

Lard for frying
Mozzarella cheese
Anchovies

With a sharp knife cut 8 slices about ¾ inch thick from fresh white bread. Cut into finger-length pieces. In a deep plate containing a little hot meat broth or gravy, moisten the pieces of bread and pour the eggs over them. Set aside to rest for at least 1 hour—2 hours if possible. Then sauté the bread slices for 10 minutes in hot lard. This gives the bread the golden crust in which it may worthily appear in a mixed fry. If the *pan dorato* is to be the highlight of the *fritto,* before moistening the bread, cut it horizontally, but not all the way through, so that it opens like a book. Put a piece of Mozzarella and a piece of anchovy inside. Then moisten the bread in the broth, pour the beaten eggs over it, and fry in the hot lard till golden brown. As the anchovies are rather salty, a second glass of Frascati would go well with this dish. Serves 4.

FRITTI DI FIORI DI ZUCCA
Fried Squash (or Pumpkin) Blossoms

When the sun beats down on the Eternal City and the shadow of the obelisk is the only cool spot on St. Peter's

Square, artichokes disappear from the *fritti* and squash blossoms take their place. Young, unopened blossoms are especially good for this *fritto*.

Unlike the other ingredients of the *fritti*, squash blossoms are not "gilded" (*dorati*) with a coating of flour and egg, but dipped in a mixture of flour and water, called *pastella*. Instead of water you may use dry (but by no means sour) white wine. Frascati is excellent in this dish.

32 to 36 young, unopened squash
   (or pumpkin) blossoms
1 cup lukewarm water (or dry
   white wine)
2 cups all-purpose flour
2 tablespoons olive oil
¾ teaspoon salt

1 egg white, stiffly beaten
1 small piece of Mozzarella
   cheese
1 small piece of ham
Oil for deep frying
Lemon wedges

Pour the liquid into the flour all at once and stir rapidly to prevent lumping and to give a smooth, flowing *pastella*, the consistency of heavy cream. Then add olive oil and salt. Let it stand for 2 hours. Just before using, fold in egg white. The *pastella* must be velvety and smooth and creamy.

Using a sharp knife, carefully slit the blossoms open and tuck a little piece of Mozzarella or a cube of ham (from Parma) inside. There is no objection to using both. Dip the blossoms into the batter (*pastella*). Sauté in hot oil until golden brown and serve with the customary lemon wedges. Serves 4.

FRITTO DI FILETTI DI ZUCCHINI
Fried Zucchini

Squash blossoms, like roses and carnations of memory-book fame, bloom and fade. When the squash blossom dies, the squash—or the smaller, softer variety called *zucchino*—appears.

1½ pounds small zucchini	All-purpose flour
1 teaspoon salt	Olive oil

Peel the zucchini, gently scoop out the inside with the seeds, and cut the rest into thin strips about 1½ to 3½ inches long. Sprinkle with salt and let them drain for several hours. When ready to use, press them between your hands, dry them on towels, and dredge with flour (shaking them in a sieve to remove superfluous flour). Fry a few at a time in deep oil that should be bubbling merrily, till the vegetables brown. Drain on brown paper or toweling and serve promptly. Serves 4. Experienced *friggitori* (vendors of fried foods) use deep pots for frying zucchini.

FRITTO DI CAVOLFIORI, BROCCOLI E FUNGHI
Fried Cauliflower, Broccoli, and Mushrooms

When squash disappears from the markets, cauliflower (*cavolfiori*) and its nearest relative, broccoli, arrive. The broccoli flower remains green, is somewhat harder than cauliflower, and has rosettes that are more like pointed shells. Cauliflower (or broccoli) is first cooked in hot water till just tender, cut into small pieces, and like the squash blossoms is then dipped in *pastella* (batter—see page 33), and fried. Slice the mushrooms and either dip them in the batter or "gild" them in flour and egg (see *Pan dorato*, pages 31–32). Serve with lemon wedges.

PESCE FRITTI
Fried Fish

Since Caesar's day the sea has retreated from Rome. The "yellow" Tiber has carried so much sand and loam to the harbor of Ostia, once the port of Rome, that today the ancient part of the old seaside town lies some distance inland. On the other hand, connections have so greatly improved that from a culinary standpoint Rome is still a city on the Mediterranean—the sea that gastronomes rank above all others because of its amazing variety of fish, crabs, and polyps.

Small to medium-sized fish are better fried, as is also the squid—in the bloom of their youth when they are no bigger than the lemons that accompany them. Whereas for all other *fritture,* lard or beef suet is permitted, fish require pure olive oil which may be heated to 550° F. (without smoking or turning black) so that the fish will be fried very quickly. There is a definite affinity between the fish of the Mediterranean and the fruit of olive trees (which perhaps might be explained by the relationship between Neptune and Minerva). It is more difficult to explain why fried squid go so well with artichokes.

Small fish are first dipped in flour, then placed in a sieve (which is shaken gently to free them of superfluous flour) and fried in boiling oil. In a few minutes they are done and crisp. Larger fish are rolled in flour, picked up by the tail and dipped briefly in cold water, which makes the flour stick better. Set the fried fish aside to dry in a warm spot on the stove. If the natural sea salt is not sufficient, salt lightly before serving.

SEPPIE (CALAMARI, CALAMARETTI) FRITTI
Fried Squid

The squid plays at least as important a part in the history of Roman literature as in the history of cookery. From the time of Ennius down to the Church Fathers every word was put on papyrus with the juice of this polyp. In Rome, therefore, the squid or "inkfish" is called "inkwell" (*calamaro*).

Squid	Olive oil
All-purpose flour	Salt to taste

First remove the dark fluid with which the *calamaro* (like many writers who use the same weapon) defends himself. Then cut the sac into rings (without opening it). These rings as well as the tentacles are then dipped in flour, freed of superfluous flour in a sieve, and fried quickly in hot olive oil till done. Only young squid may be prepared in this simple fashion. Older squid are tough and must be fried slowly.

As the sea gives up squid year in and year out the rings, which seem so mysterious to the inland dweller, are often found in a *fritto misto*.

BACCALÀ FRITTO
Fried Salt Cod

Why the Romans give cod a place of honor on the bill of fare is not easy to understand. Perhaps because once upon a time the fishermen along the coast from Civitavecchia to Anzio could not supply them with enough fish, and the "Romani" of past centuries—in contrast to those of today—would not risk their souls by eating a roast chicken on Friday; perhaps only because a properly cooked codfish tastes so good.

Salt codfish (about 3 pounds)
1 cup all-purpose flour
½ cup lukewarm water (or dry
    white wine)

2 tablespoons olive oil
1 egg white, stiffly beaten
Olive oil for frying
Lemon slices

Place the codfish in water for 24 hours, changing it several times to wash away the salt. But if the cooked fish still causes strong thirst, the visitor to Rome has the red and white wines of the "Castelli Romani" at his disposal.

Remove the bones from the softened fish and cut it into strips 1½ to 2½ inches long by about 1 inch wide. Pour the water or wine into flour all at once and stir rapidly to prevent lumping and to give a smooth flowing batter. Add oil, let stand 2 hours. Just before using fold in egg white. Dip the strips in batter and fry them in moderately hot oil. The fried codfish is served accompanied by the usual lemon wedges, but never as a part of a mixed fry. Serves 4 to 5.

CROCCHETTE DI POLLO
Chicken Croquettes

Chicken croquettes apparently came to Rome by way of France, which, considering the long, though not always untroubled, relations between Rome and Paris, is not surprising, especially as croquettes fit excellently into the list of *fritti*. Béchamel sauce, which is the basis of the recipe, is further proof of its transalpine origin. Linguistically minded Italian patriots call it *besciamella* sauce.

½ cup butter
1 cup all-purpose flour
1½ teaspoons salt
¼ teaspoon pepper
Nutmeg
1½ cups milk

⅓ cup grated Parmesan cheese
2 cups ground or chopped cooked
    chicken or rabbit meat
Fine dry bread crumbs
1 egg, well beaten
Fat for deep frying

Melt butter in top part of double boiler or heavy saucepan. Remove from heat. Blend in flour, salt, pepper, and a pinch of nutmeg. Add milk, return to heat, and cook until very thick. Add chicken (or rabbit) and cheese. The Parmesan cheese distinguishes the Roman croquette from croquettes made elsewhere. When the mixture has cooled, spread it out on a board that has been dredged with flour and bread crumbs and shape it into round, small flat cakes or little finger-thick sticks. These are then dipped in egg and fried a beautiful brown in medium hot deep fat. You may also add to the croquette minced ham, cooked mushrooms, truffles from Norcia, or simply a little parsley. Serves 4.

ꞁꞁ PASTASCIUTTA
Spaghetti, Macaroni, Noodles, etc.

Very dogmatic persons will deny *pastasciutta* the right
to Roman citizenship. "Spaghetti, macaroni, etc.," they say,
"are a discovery of the nineteenth century. Moreover they
entered the city through the breach in the Porta Pia." On the
other hand, it is true that the modern inhabitant of the City
on the Seven Hills cannot imagine life without *pastasciutta*,
his beloved spaghetti. If we divide the peninsula from the
standpoint of carbohydrates, the Province of Venetia is a
polenta (cornmeal) section, rice reigns north of the Po, while
south of it *pastasciutta* has practically captured all palates—
even though it is no longer equally well prepared in all
places. Bologna, for example, makes aromatic and particularly
nourishing sauces and ragouts for its spaghetti; Florence, on
the other hand, is completely without imagination in this
respect. The city of Leonardo and Michelangelo excels chiefly
in its beefsteak, *bistecca florentina*, which is indeed unsurpassed for tenderness. But if in no other way, Rome proves
by the number of its *sughi* (sauces) that give the *pastasciutta* color and character that it is the capital of Italy. This
angers Neapolitans, who once had a king of their own. They

39

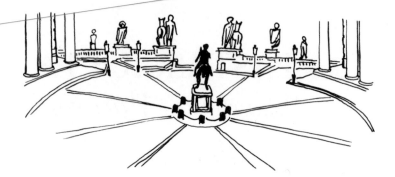

point out, quite rightly, that the first *pastasciutta* was made in Naples around the year 1800 and was dried in the steady temperature of volcanic hollows and caves. They also maintain that sauces with eggplant, mussels, and fish are far the best. As the ancient Romans decreed that *de gustibus* was not a subject for debate, we will not go into that argument.

Certain it is, however, that *pastasciutta* made its appearance only a few centuries ago—and the Italians of today are more surprised at this than anyone else. "Isn't it as old as bread?" they ask in amazement. And, "But what did people eat in those days?" People ate bread—the ancient bread that perhaps Adam learned to bake in paradise, for without bread it would not have been paradise. The cooks of ancient days racked their brains to invent syrups and sauces to accompany bread, the very sauces of which Apicius recorded 138—certainly only a small portion of them.

Dry bread? Fine, when you have it, but with something on it, it is much better. Butter was unknown in ancient Rome (the word *butyros* is Greek) and the problem of "Butter or javelins" did not exist. Most of the citizens seldom saw meat. Wood and coal were equally scarce; the charcoal stove was a luxury for aristocratic houses, but was altogether unknown in the tenement houses in which the poor taxpayers—the *misera plebs contribuens*—lived. When the poor had nothing else to eat, they dipped their bread in vinegar; when life was easier, they dipped it in vinegar and oil. On special occasions they crushed bay leaves, rue, savory, and all sorts of aromatic herbs in the dish that stood in the center of the table between the guests. They may even have added a peppercorn that, after a journey from the ends of the earth, had rolled from the table of a patrician. They learned—the centuries are excellent teachers—to make a sauce (*succus*) from a bit of meat, a little wine, oil, vinegar, and a few herbs. Since those days the introduction of the tomato from Peru has brought about a great change in the *sughi*.

The Neapolitans prefer fish and mussels in their sauces and in this they are simply continuing an old and noble tradition. In the days of the Caesars *garum*, so often mentioned by Apicius, was frequently found on the table. Apicius states that it was served weak or sharp—as *hydrogarum* or *oxygarum*. That *garum* was some sort of a fish sauce was known, but archaeologists admitted that they were unable to reconstruct the recipe.

The secret was first disclosed in 1960 when during excavations at Herculaneum a vase bearing the inscription "GARUM" was unearthed. Scholars from the famous aquarium in Naples easily established that the bones and heads found in the vase were from herring and salmon—a discovery that, at long last, perhaps explained why Julius Caesar marched to the mouth of the Rhine and to Britain!

The ancient idea of serving a farinaceous dish with many different sauces gained fresh importance when, toward the end of the eighteenth century, the first fine flour sieves were manufactured and one could make white bread in large quantities (Napoleon's armies were the first in the world to have white bread). Whether the first *pastasciutta* was introduced in Naples during Murat's reign or whether an invention from Sardinia was first brought to the mainland, not even the great

Italian encyclopedia (Treccani) can tell us. It is certain, however, that the Sardinians made fine flour sieves by pulling out
every second thread from woven silk. Now, the last direct
descendants of the Etruscans, who for their part (so it seems
to me) were pure Hittites, still live in Sardinia today. It is,
therefore, altogether possible that in the happy union of *pasta-*

sciutta and sauce, two traditions thousands of years old have
been joined.

Perhaps that ancient background explains the swift tri-
umphal march of *pastasciutta* throughout the peninsula Gari-
baldi united. Rome itself clung as firmly to grain as it clung
to the foundations of power and culture, with the result that
it looked upon potatoes and corn with mistrust (at best the
potato goes into the oven with the roast lamb, corn appears
in winter as an excuse to stand long hours in front of the warm
stove and stir *polenta*). With all the more enthusiasm, therefore, Romans welcomed anything that gave their sauces a new
color. The tomato quickly won citizenship and in time no one
could think of a day when the beautiful red color had not
appeared on one's plate.

That Rome chose the third of three farinaceous dishes,
rice, corn, *pastasciutta,* is probably because it is so easy to
prepare. The climate of Rome is somehow not conducive to
hard work. Even in the first thousand years the Romans pre-

ferred to plunder rather than plow, and when there was nothing left to plunder their difficulties began. The empire fell, but then came Christianity, and Peter's pence rolled in, now sparsely, now abundantly, but always toward Rome even when the city had nothing to supply but occasional relics. That safe and not overly strenuous existence seemed threatened for a moment when the Red Shirts came . . . but only for a very brief moment. The Red Shirts brought the Ministry Offices to Rome; vast structures sprouted like tumors, in which no one exhausted himself with work. The Black Shirts did almost the same thing: they brought in a party system that meant steady jobs and good wages for the friends of good cooking who were so in need of rest. A million Romans—or are there more?—are living today on government jobs and because Peter's successor pastures his sheep and guards his lambs. They do not live poorly.

Pastasciutta, which is easily prepared, found the right climate in Rome. But nothing is so simple that it cannot go wrong. We must therefore set forth certain basic principles here.

Difficult as it may appear, it is quite possible, with the help of a simple fork, to carry the long spaghetti strips to your mouth without spattering your clothes, the tablecloth, and your neighbor with sauce. Little four-year-old Romans are able to do it with ease. The difficulties of eating *pastasciutta* are not to be compared with playing the piano, though to be sure on your first attempt you must exercise a bit of patience. But to call angrily for a knife and to cut the spaghetti and eat it with a spoon is exactly what one must not do in restaurants if one doesn't wish to be considered a barbarian. In the same way the inflexible rules of cookery strictly forbid breaking the spaghetti, no matter how long it is, and tossing it in little pieces into the water.

And it is just as strictly forbidden to "cool" the hot spaghetti with cold water. Anyone who commits such sins will be looked at askance, just as if a man in fox-hunting England announced that he had shot foxes with a gun. Anyone who cuts fish with a knife can still count on forgiveness; but the man who cuts or breaks *pastasciutta* and pours cold water over it is damned.

It is a fatal mistake for the cook to pour off the water from the pasta too soon—or too late. And woe to him who tries to settle this question with the clock in his hand! By the sea, water boils at 212° F., and on higher ground at lower temperatures. In the Holy Father's villa at Castel Gandolfo spaghetti for the pontifical table must be cooked somewhat longer than in the Vatican, especially in the reign of His Holiness John XXIII, who was a connoisseur. The cooking time depends naturally on the thickness of the individual pieces of pasta.

The trick with spaghetti, macaroni, etc. (if you are using brands bought in Italian stores) is to slip the spaghetti gradually by handfuls (holding it by the top) into the boiling water so as not to stop it from boiling. Then, after you have slipped the pasta into the boiling water—the heat must be high enough for it to start boiling again at once—you must pay the closest attention and concentrate on your work. To

cook *pastasciutta* and meanwhile make the sauce, listen to the radio and discuss important family matters with your neighbor across the alley, is practically impossible. You must watch carefully for the precise moment when the spaghetti begins to soften. When that critical moment approaches, take out a strand of spaghetti and taste it. . . . Then, with all the sensitiveness of the violinist who listens closely as he tunes his instrument, you must decide, by tasting, whether it is "done" or "not yet done."

Factories in Naples (and in America) put out a pasta that is somewhat cheaper, but boils soft quickly. The pasta from the factories in the north of Italy is more expensive, but it cooks better and retains a firm consistency (*al dente*—so that you feel it under your teeth) even when it cooks one minute overtime.*

However, no Roman housewife would dare to put the spaghetti into boiling water until the expected guest was in the house. If he should be ten minutes late, he might be served an overcooked or a cold, sticky pasta which would be

* There are excellent brands of spaghetti, macaroni, etc., on the American market. They may be purchased in any good grocery store.

"inconceivable." Not until the whole family, including the guest, are gathered together will the password be given: *Butto giù la pasta*—I'm tossing in the pasta. The ten or fifteen minutes' wait will then be rewarded by a *pastasciutta come Dio comanda* (*pastasciutta* as God commands).

While it is impossible to give the exact cooking time, it is equally difficult to say how much *pastasciutta* to reckon per person. One hero made the world record by eating six pounds. A restaurant portion consists of 5¼ ounces, which is sufficient if fish, meat, vegetables, coffee, cheese, and fruit are served afterwards.

A third factor which is difficult to express in words, is the importance of the shape of the dough from which the *pasta-sciutta* is to be made. The *Enciclopedia Italiana* states firmly —and no one will deny it—"It is a fact that, when the same mass of dough from the same factory is molded in various shapes, each shape has a different taste." We leave it to wiser men to explain the phenomenon. Perhaps someday a chemist will write a definitive treatise on the surface absorption of fatty sauces in softened dough. We shall merely report that there

are "long" and "short" pasta; that the long spaghetti comes in various widths, that the tube-shaped variety often called macaroni (*maccheroni*) is seldom eaten in Rome. Among the "short" types, the thick tubes of *rigatoni* are the most important, as they are eaten with *pagliata* (steamed small intestine of beef). *Bucatini,* which are similarly shaped but smaller, go well with bean soup.

I SUGHI
Sauces (*for* pastasciutta)

"*Variatio delectat,*" said the old Romans—variety gives pleasure. Whether this charming sentence, which children are given for practice of the third declension, comes from cookery or from philosophy we do not know. But that the principle (which Frenchmen later illustrated with the instructive story *toujours perdrix*) is valid in cookery, Marcus Gavius Apicius proved personally, though he had certainly not made a note of all the well-seasoned sauces of his day. Who knows what was lost when the basic works on Greek cookery were burned in the library of Alexandria! How much we could learn if the excavations brought to light a copy of the *Deipnologia* (Dietetics) by Archestratus, that much praised man who traveled through all the ancient world "to give pleasure to the stomach and what lies below it."

The northerner, with his meals of herring and potatoes, the Brazilian who, year in and year out, lives on rice and black beans, console themselves with the thought that the Italian has his *pastasciutta* every day. Far from it! Every day in the year, 365 different *sughi* enrich a new dish on his table.

Future archaeologists, scholars who attempt to reconstruct our age from books, will scarcely be able to picture this great

variety. Excellent cookbooks break down before the attempt. A fine cookbook of 800 pages lies in my kitchen. It mentions 50 sauces for meat and only 10 *sughi* (*sauces for pastasciutta*), among them several varieties of purely local importance.

The omission is understandable: the young Italian woman does not learn the art of making sauces from books; she learns it from her mother, the neighbor, a friend, at the last and in the greatest detail from her mother-in-law, and—this is the important part—when she knows the basic principles, she improvises. Beethoven's contemporaries insisted that his improvisations were far superior to his written works. It is a tragedy for mankind that so many sonatas and *sughi*, the result of a momentary flash of genius, are irretrievably lost for all time!

Rule 1: in preparing *sugo,* the *sugo* can wait for the pasta, but not vice versa. When the spaghetti is cooked and ready to be served, the *sugo* must be ready and waiting.

Rule 2: it is impossible to give the exact amount of the ingredients. Whether more or less butter, ham, or cheese are added to the dish depends upon the hostess's resources. "The difference between the king and me," the Neapolitan used to say in the days when he had a king, "is that the king eats as much *pastasciutta* as he wants and I eat as much as I have." The same rule applies to the *sugo* that ennobles the pasta. In wartime the trick was to dress up a sauce with homeopathic doses of doubtful fat, with bay leaves and cabbage leaves gathered in the public gardens (instead of flowers, as we have mentioned, cabbages were planted there, and between the cabbage heads stood small tablets bearing the inscription: "We shall win.") On the other hand, in peacetime or prewar days we were told to resist the delights of the *uncta popina,* the fleshpots rich in fat. But now, as is customary in scholarly works, we shall list the main ingredients of the *sughi* for the benefit of the neophyte in Roman cookery:

Fats: Olive oil, pork rind, bacon, the fat from smoked ham, butter, fat drippings from meat.

Meat: Little pieces of meat of all sorts, poultry, meat juices, stew meat, raw ham, cooked ham, sausages.

Seafood: Tuna, anchovies, mussels.

Seasonings (also called *odori,* fragrances): Parsley, marjoram, rosemary, basil, celery, sage, grated carrots, onions, garlic, leeks, scallions.

Vegetables: Peppers, peas, fresh tomatoes, peeled and seeded tomatoes, *conserva* (tomato paste), and whole canned tomatoes.

For special sauces you may add: Wine, eggs, mushrooms, truffles, lemons, cream.

A mathematician can prove that out of these ingredients a housewife can make enough different *sughi*, without once repeating, to last from the time of her honeymoon to her silver wedding anniversary. But before we begin to fan the coals and set out our *sugo*, we must answer another question: are pasta and *sugo* mixed in the pan before serving or only on the plate at the table?

Women with many children will doubtless choose the first method—also with the idea of saving the tablecloth. But if you have made a special *sugo* in honor of a dear guest, it is better to serve it in a special earthenware or porcelain dish and let the guest prepare the final step himself. Before serving stir a little piece of butter into the pasta and mix well to prevent it from being sticky. The amount of freshly ground cheese to be used is left to the guest's discretion.

Cheeses from two localities were providentially chosen to appear with the pasta on the table: *pecorino* and *parmigiano* (Parmesan). *Pecorino* is a ripe hard sheep's cheese which is made in small 1½- to 2-kilogram heavy molds in the Abruzzi and in Sardinia. It has a sharp spicy taste and up to the turn of the century was unrivaled in Roman cookery. Today it is generally mixed with Parmesan. Foreigners, and many Ro-

mans, prefer the milder Parmesan made from cow's milk. It is turned out in tremendous heavy forms, ripens for two years before it is given the title *vecchio* (old), longer to receive the crowning title *stravecchio* (very old). It must be grated just before using if its special quality is to be savored.

A final word in these general directions: cheese does not belong on all *sughi!* Pasta accompanied by products of the sea, such as tuna fish and mussels, is always served without cheese. . . . If you want to hide cheese *under* the *sugo* you may—but the greatest part must be sprinkled on top of the *sugo*. It is the crowning touch.

CON BURRO E FORMAGGIO "IN BIANCO"
With Butter and Cheese "in White"

Italian folk therapy still clings to the old belief that red food and dark brown food are warming, white food is cooling. That is why people ill with fever are served their spaghetti (or its thinnest type, *vermicelli* or "little worms") entirely *in bianco*. There is no reason why the healthy—perhaps with better appetites—cannot enjoy this dish too.

The spaghetti, cooked and drained, is mixed with fresh butter while still hot and dredged generously with grated Parmesan. A simple variant: use browned butter instead of cold creamed butter.

CON AGLIO, OLIO E PEPERONCINO
With Garlic, Oil, Hot Red Peppers

The garlic (2-3 cloves for each dish) is sliced, browned lightly in oil, and then immediately removed from the pan.

Next crush a hot red pepper in oil. Before serving, and as you take the pan off the heat, scatter finely chopped parsley over it. There is no cheese in this pasta.

ALL' AMATRICIANA
The Way the Women of Amatrice Prepare It

Amatrice is a picturesque little town in the Abruzzi. As it is not known to every tourist (nor to every cookbook author either), it is now and then misspelled and written *"alla matriciana."* Not even such a blunder can spoil the flavor that results from this method of cooking, which is especially popular in Rome.

1 onion, sliced thinly
¾ cup diced fat smoked ham
Oil
2½ pounds fresh tomatoes, peeled and seeded

Salt and pepper
Pecorino and Parmesan as desired

Cook onion with the ham and oil until onion is golden. Add the tomatoes and cook until they are soft but not overcooked. Salt and pepper to taste. Serves 4.

Romans, true to tradition, sprinkle it lightly with grated *pecorino,* liberally with Parmesan.

Giggi Fazi, the Roman chef, published a variation which we shall repeat literally here. It is as much a test of the difference between the Tuscan and the Roman speech as it is proof of how culinary ideas may be embodied in various forms.

Hostaria Romana
by Giggi Fazi

Li bucatini a la matriciana': 'Nde na' padella ce metti 'n goccio d'ojo, 'na 'nticchi de peperoncino, de guanciale

affumicato tajato a tocchetti. Quanno è arosolato l'am-
morbidisci cor vino bianco 'n tre vorte, poi ce schiaffi er
pomidoro e fai coce pe' sette minuti. Coci li bucatini ar
dente e acconnisci cor sugo e pecorino.

"Put a little oil in the pan, with a piece of sweet pepper
and bacon, diced. When this has cooked, soften it three
times with white wine, then throw in the tomatoes and
cook seven minutes longer. Cook the *bucatini al dente*
(so that they do not become too soft) and serve them
with sauce and *pecorino* cheese."

ALLA POVERELLA
The Way the Poor Woman Makes It

Pork rind or bacon	Pepper
Spaghetti, cooked	Cheese to taste
2 eggs	

Dice pork rind or bacon and try it out over high heat. Toss
the drained cooked spaghetti into the pan, stir until it is
soaked with the hot fat, then beat the eggs into the spaghetti
mixture one at a time. Pepper generously (there is usually
enough salt in the bacon) and cook slowly 2-5 minutes longer
until the spaghetti, covered with a smooth coating of egg,
is as beautifully yellow as an egg yolk. Tastes delicious with
or without cheese.

Pasta alla poverella is a specialty of the *trattorie* in Trastevere (the part of the city on the right bank of the Tiber)
such as, for instance, the Antica Pesa. The host expects the
guest to ask: "But why *alla poverella?* Bacon and eggs are
dear enough!" Then the host, looking as if he were betraying
a secret, replies: "The name comes from the days when eggs
were still cheap!"

COL SUGO DI POMODORI FRESCHI
With Fresh Tomato Juice

2½ pounds fresh tomatoes   1 tablespoon butter
Salt   Parmesan cheese to taste
Parsley

This sauce is especially recommended to those who have eaten too much *pasta alla poverella* the day before.

The tomatoes are cooked down in a very small amount of water, then rubbed through a fine sieve. Simmer the juice over low heat till thick, add salt to taste and a little finely chopped parsley. When you pour the sauce over the pasta, add butter. This may be served with or without Parmesan.

CON POMODORI E PEPERONI
With Tomatoes and Sweet Peppers

6 large sweet peppers (yellow or   2 pounds fresh tomatoes, seeded
  red)   and peeled
2 onions, sliced   Salt
½ cup oil (or half butter, half   Pepper
  oil)

The thick-fleshed yellow or red peppers are best quartered lengthwise and emptied of seeds. Sauté in oil with the onions. When they are almost soft, add the tomatoes. Salt and pepper to taste. Cook 15 minutes more by which time the sauce will be thickened. Mix with cooked spaghetti and serve without cheese. Serves 4.

CON LE ACCIUGHE
With Anchovies

½ cup boned and chopped
   anchovies
½ cup olive oil

½ teaspoon pepper
2 pounds fresh tomatoes,
   quartered

Put anchovies in olive oil with pepper and heat. When they are warm, add tomatoes, peeled and seeded (one 6-ounce can of tomato paste and 3 cans water or 3½ cups canned whole tomatoes may be used). Simmer sauce until thick. There is enough salt in the anchovies; the spaghetti that is to be covered with this sauce may also be cooked in unsalted water. Serves 4.

COL TONNO
With Tuna Fish

3 anchovies	Salt
2 tablespoons olive oil	Pepper
1 can tomato paste (6 ounces)	Marjoram
1 can tuna (about 7 ounces, un-drained)	Chopped parsley
	Mushrooms (optional)

Tuna from a can is the basis for this sauce. In this case the anchovies are chopped fine and drenched in olive oil. As soon as the oil is hot stir in tomato paste and thin it with 3 cans water. Tuna follows and is mixed with the sauce. Season with salt, pepper, marjoram, or parsley to taste. You may also add cooked or canned mushrooms. Spaghetti with tuna is always served without cheese and may be eaten hot or (in the evening) cold. Serves 4.

CON LA CARNE
With Meat

1 onion	Juices from braised or steamed
3 tablespoons oil	meat (see pages 102–104)
3 tablespoons butter	A piece of cooked meat or cheese
½ clove garlic	as desired
1 can tomato paste (6 ounces)	

Slice one onion very thin and brown it in olive oil and butter. Sauté garlic with it, but remove it from the pan before it is quite brown. Then add the tomato paste and immediately afterward the meat juices, plus enough water to fill paste can 3 times. A finely chopped piece of the meat itself is a good addition to this *sugo*. It is unnecessary to add salt, pepper or herbs, as the meat juices contain all those ingredients.

A generous helping of cheese adds to the taste and "hides"

the fatty content so that even those who are worried about their figure may enjoy larger portions. (Or: Skim fat from sauce or chill sauce and then remove fat. Reheat before serving.) Serves 4.

COL CACIO E PEPE
With Cheese and pepper

To compensate for the preceding recipe, this is a fat-free *pastasciutta*. After cooking the spaghetti as usual, do not drain off all the water in which it is cooked, but reserve a little of the water. This will keep the spaghetti from sticking together. Sprinkle generously with grated cheese (*pecorino* if you want to keep up tradition, Parmesan if you prefer to follow the newer style) and just as generously with pepper. The guest may be permitted to correct the taste by adding 1 or 2 tablespoons of olive oil (and in that case to postpone his reducing cure till the next day).

CON LE TELLINE
With Little Mussels

Whereas Roman cookery claims *sugo* with *telline* as its specialty, Neapolitan cookery boasts of its *sughi* with *vongole*. The difference is purely linguistic: the little yellowish mussels that are found along the shores of the Mediterranean at ebb tide are called by a different name every thirty miles.

About ¾ pound mussels per person	2 small tomatoes per person
4 tablespoons olive oil	Pepper
1 clove garlic, sliced	Parsley

Scrub mussel shells thoroughly. To open the mussels, put them in a pan with a tablespoonful of olive oil, cover and set them over heat for a few minutes, or until mussels open. When the mussels are opened, remove from shell and discard the "beard" from each. There will be a little sea water left in the pot (aside from the olive oil) that tastes of mussels. It would be a pity to throw it away. Strain it through a piece of cheese-cloth—or a clean white cloth—to free it of sand, and set it aside. Olive oil definitely belongs to this *sugo*. Heat 3 table-spoons oil and add garlic. Cook till it is golden, then remove. Now add fresh, peeled and seeded tomatoes or the same amount of canned whole tomatoes. To end with, add the mussels and the mussel water. Pepper to taste and sprinkle with chopped parsley. This dish must be cooked quickly, for the flesh of the mussel is soft. Serve without cheese.

CON BASILICO
With Basil

Basil is a little plant that can be easily grown in the garden or even better in a flower pot. It will not stand frost. With tomato salad there is nothing better than basil; on the Ligurian coast no *sugo* is served without it.

⅔ cup diced bacon
1 clove garlic
¼ cup chopped parsley
2 tablespoons butter
1 can tomato paste (6 ounces)
   or 2 pounds fresh tomatoes, chopped

Water or beef bouillon
2 tablespoons minced basil
   leaves
Salt and pepper

Sauté bacon, garlic, and parsley in butter over high heat. When bacon is lightly browned add tomato paste thinned with

2 cans water or bouillon. Fresh tomatoes are better than canned. Before serving add basil leaves and salt and pepper to taste. Serves 4.

COL REGAGLIE DI POLLO
With Chicken Livers and Hearts

½ cup butter, or half butter and
    half oil
1 onion, sliced
6 chicken livers and hearts,
    chopped
1½ cups chopped boiled chicken

1 carrot, grated
1 stalk celery, chopped
1 can tomato paste (6 ounces)
Chicken broth
Salt, pepper, and parsley as de-
    sired

In ½ cup butter—or half butter and half oil—brown onion lightly, then add livers, hearts, and chicken, carrot, celery, tomato paste, and 3 paste cans of chicken broth. Cover and cook over high heat till thickened (about 35 minutes). The pieces of heart will then be tender. Salt, pepper, and parsley to taste. Serves 4.

CON I PISELLI
With peas

The peas of the Roman Campagna are the tenderest in the world. Cooked quickly over high heat, they will be tender in 10 minutes. They make a perfect combination with raw ham from Parma. (Prosciutto can be bought in America in any Italian grocery and many specialty shops.)

1 onion, sliced
1 celery stalk
Parsley
1 slice bacon
2 tablespoons olive oil
¼ pound raw ham (prosciutto)

Pepper
2 cups shelled fresh peas
¼ cup meat broth, canned beef
 bouillon, or water
Tomato paste, as desired
Parmesan cheese, as desired

Spread onion, celery, and a little parsley on a slice of bacon. Using a sharp knife, chop all very fine. This mixture is cooked down in olive oil till soft, then add the lean raw ham which you have cut into strips. As a rule it is not necessary to add salt, but a little pepper does no harm. Then add the peas and broth, bouillon, or water. Cover and cook gently for 10 minutes, at which time the peas will be tender and the *sugo* done. Add more liquid if necessary. To give the broth a nice color you may add a little tomato paste. Excellent with or without Parmesan cheese. Serves 4.

CON LA SALSICCIA
With Sausage

Even sausages are different north and south of the Alps. Those that come to Rome from the Abruzzi, especially in winter, are so generously supplied with salt, pepper, and herbs that it is easy to make a spicy *sugo* out of them.

1 onion, sliced
2 tablespoons butter or olive oil
1 pound sausage
½ cup dry white wine

1 can tomato paste (6 ounces),
 if desired
Grated cheese

Cook onion in hot butter or olive oil. Empty contents of sausage skins and add. The meat will be browned in a few minutes. Now pour in wine (dry Frascati or Marino or any good dry white wine) and let *sugo* cook. The *sugo* is then

ready—unless you wish to add tomato paste thinned with 2 cans water and cook it another 5 minutes. This will not only give you the desired red coloring, but also make it easier to mix with the spaghetti. Serve with plenty of grated cheese. Serves 4.

CON I FUNGHI
With Mushrooms

Mushrooms (*funghi porcini* or *ovoli*) and truffles (*tartufi*) are good additions to many varieties of *sughi*. Tuna goes excellently cooked with the mushrooms called *porcini*—spaghetti with anchovies is far more impressive if black truffles from Umbria are sprinkled over it like cheese, when it is cooked. But even mushrooms alone make an excellent and quickly prepared *sugo*. Cut 1 pound mushrooms in slices, sauté in ⅓ cup butter or olive till soft and the water from the

mushrooms has evaporated. Finish with a sprinkling of lemon
juice, salt, pepper, and a little parsley. Serves 4.

COL MASCARPONE
With Mascarpone Cheese

The tourist who leaves Rome without tasting the creamy
mascarpone cheese can only hope that the pennies he tossed
in the Fontana di Trevi will soon bring him back again.

On his return he must not fail to seize the first opportunity
to eat his *pastasciutta* with butter and *mascarpone*. When the
pasta is cooked and drained, butter and *mascarpone* are allowed to soften in the warmth of the pasta and need no
further cooking—or words of recommendation. It is an excellent idea to mix a little minced cooked ham with the *mascarpone* before serving.

COL RAGU D'AGNELLO
With Lamb Ragout

Though Rome's place as *caput mundi*—leader of the
world—is not altogether uncontested, the peasants of the
Abruzzi have always considered, and still consider, Rome as
"their" capital. Ever since Ovid, himself an Abruzzese, came
down from his mountains to the city, peasants of the Abruzzi
have been coming with lambs to the Pantheon. . . . In the
little *trattorie* in the Pantheon district, which are among the
best purveyors of Roman cookery, they find their favorite
sugo:

1 pound boneless lamb	4 fresh tomatoes, peeled and
2 tablespoons oil	seeded
2 tablespoons butter	Salt
3 large green peppers	Pepper
½ cup Frascati (or any dry white wine)	

The lamb meat is cut in small pieces and sautéed till brown in half oil and half butter, to which are added peppers cut in lengthwise strips. Add wine, cover and simmer slowly over low heat. When the meat is tender, add tomatoes, peeled and seeded, and allow them to cook down. Salt and pepper to taste complete this masterpiece. Serves 4.

AL RAGU
With Ragout

If pasta itself came to Rome from the South, the ragout came from the North and especially from Bologna. The two met in Rome and particularly enjoy meeting on Sundays. On weekdays *pasta al ragù* is prepared only for special guests who know how to appreciate this honor.

½ pound lean beef	Parmesan cheese
¼ pound bacon	4 chicken livers
1 onion	¼ cup chopped raw ham
1 carrot	½ pound fresh mushrooms,
Parsley	chopped
1 small clove garlic	Small amount minced sausage,
½ cup butter	goose liver, or cooked tongue
2 tablespoons meat juices or broth	(optional)
	Cream
1 tablespoon tomato paste	Truffles

Chop the beef very fine with bacon, onion, carrot, a little parsley, and garlic (or if, in spite of doubt as to modern technical progress in the art of Apicius, you wish to save time, put all these ingredients through the meat grinder). Cook the mixture in 6 tablespoons of butter until it is a beautiful dark brown. Then add 1 tablespoon of meat juices or broth, tomato paste, and then another tablespoon of meat juices. Let this simmer very slowly. When it is done, add a little grated Parmesan cheese, which gives this dish the special touch that marks a feast day. Meanwhile in another pan simmer gently in 2 tablespoons of butter, till tender, chicken livers, raw ham, sliced mushrooms, and, if available, sausage, tongue, or goose liver. When the ragout has been on the stove a good half hour and the kitchen is filled with its fragrant aroma (travelers who know Italy notice from this aroma in the air that their express train is stopping at Bologna) then combine the contents of both pans. For very important occasions cream and thinly sliced truffles may be added at the end. Serves 4.

Remarks about *Sughi*

Twenty *sughi* present only a vague picture of the many possibilities; in the space of this little book we cannot hope to give a complete list. But anyone who learns to make them all and has tasted them will have gained enough skill and experience to discover further possibilities on his own, perhaps even to begin to improvise. Moreover, anyone who learns several of these recipes by heart will find the entree to Rome's citizenship that others, less fortunate, are denied. He will be surrounded by friends.

An exchange of thoughts is always fraught with dangers on all sides. Whether the conversation turns on politics, the surest way to heaven, the usefulness of atomic power or birth control, one runs the danger of stirring up a storm. Friendly human relations are possible only by sticking to certain subjects. In their diplomatic wisdom, the English have discovered that the weather is an ideal and inexhaustible topic of conversation. As nothing can be done about it, the men who like cold and snow will listen calmly to those who make a plea for hot July days. Everyone can tell about a fog or a hailstorm such as no one else ever saw. Comparing the weather in Bermuda with the weather in Helsinki gives world travelers a chance to open new horizons to their fellow countrymen. And, most important of all, a difference in class is no deterrent to a conversation. As long as the member of the House of Lords has a subject about which he can talk pleasantly with the unemployed street sweeper, democracy is safe.

The Roman is not interested in weather. If he is caught in a downpour (*lo sgrullone*) he steps under the arch of a gate and curses, exactly as his great-grandfather used to curse under pontifical rule, and he himself under the Fascist regime: "*Porco governo ladro!*—Rotten weather! It's the fault of this crooked government!" That was not a dangerous remark, for everyone knew the weather depended on St. Peter alone and not on his deputy, or on the man whom one deputy called "the Man of Providence." A police spy (and among ten men who take refuge from the rain there is certain to be one spy) could not arrest a man for repeating a popular joke—even though he was actually expressing his own opinion about the government!

On the subject of *sughi*, therefore, you can be sure you will not offend the man with whom you are talking. The man who likes his pasta with garlic, oil, and peppers—and I admit that I belong to this group—will have complete understanding for the arguments of his opponent who prefers his pasta with butter and cheese. The conservative friends of *pecorino* find a basis for discussion with the progressive-minded Parmesan enthusiasts. Regional differences, as a rule so sharp, disappear. The Sicilian will praise his pasta seasoned with fennel and with or without anchovies, and no one will contradict him. The Genoese will explain why, at the noon hour, his home town reeks of garlic and basil; the Neapolitan, whose dialect already marks him as an expert, will declare that only tomatoes ripened in July are worthy to accompany the pasta and that there should also be some eggplant (*melanzana*) or that the *sugo* must at least be cooked in an iron pot in the same fat in which, days before, the eggplant was cooked. The man from Norcia will have something interesting to say about grated or sliced black truffles and their numerous uses; a Piedmontese will talk about the difference between the dark truffles of Umbria and the light, more pungent truffles of his home . . . and so the conversation goes gaily on. Here, too, as in the Englishman's meteorological game, class distinction plays no part. The aristocrat can talk about a recipe that has been handed down in his family and at the same time mention the part his ancestors played in the Crusades. A much-traveled waiter is never at a loss for a contribution to the conversation, and can talk just as interestingly about customs in the Wild West and the culinary barbarians who cook pasta in *sugo* and sell it in tin cans.

The conversation takes a particularly exciting turn (in a conversation between men, not among women around a coffee table) when new methods of preparation are discussed. (The Indian troops of the British Eighth Army in World War II made a *sugo* of oil, onions, bay leaves, whole peppercorns, and plenty of curry!) Recipes are written down in notebooks and new variations suggested.

The stranger is willingly given the floor so long as he sticks to general principles—which is why I recommend that the Roman visitor study the little collection of choices. His position could then be shaken only if he should suggest cooking spaghetti in milk till soft—as one unlucky northerner once did. The daily press reported the case of a foreign woman who announced that she always soaked spaghetti in cold water the evening before she cooked it! On another occasion the philosopher Benedetto Croce voiced a shattering opinion of a man who suggested serving pasta with *raw* tomatoes. But how truly pasta can bridge antagonisms no one has shown so beautifully as Trilussa, the last great Roman dialect poet, in his poem, *La Politica*.

LA POLITICA

Ner modo de pensà c'è un gran divario;
Mi' padre è democratico cristiano,
e siccome è impiegato ar Vaticano,
tutte le sere recita er rosario;
de tre fratelli, Giggi ch'è er più anziano
è socialista rivoluzionario,
io invece so' monarchico, ar contrario
de Ludovico ch'è repubblicano.

Prima di cena liticamo spesso
pe' via de 'sti principì benedetti:
chi vò qua, chi vò là . . . Pure un congresso!

Famo l'ira de Dio! Ma appena mamma
ce dice che so' cotti li spaghetti
semo tutti d'accordo ner programma.

POLITICS

It's very strange and more than curious
That family arguments can grow so furious
Then, all of a sudden, become so spurious.

My father's a Christian Democrat
Who knows what's what and says that's that,

He's employed at the Vatican, fond of causerie
And every evening tells his rosary.

My brother Giggi spouts Socialist theories
And hurls his arguments about in wild series,
While Ludovico snorts Republican objections,
And takes his brother apart, in sections.

As for me, I'm a Monarchist, of course,
And proud of it, too—without remorse.
But when we come to the family table,
With each of us shouting as loud as he's able,
All this fighting seems less than petty
For at this point Mama brings in the spaghetti! *

Instead of *pastasciutta* serve any or all of the following—
on special occasions.

Fettuccine (thin noodles), *gnocchi* (potato noodles or
dumplings), *agnolotti* (ravioli, little cases made of pasta
dough), *gnocchi di semolino* (grits noodles), *polenta* (cornmeal), or *timballo* (pasta or rice with eggs in a mold).

No matter how many different ways *pastasciutta* is served,
it is always only a variation of the same basic recipe. As
everyone likes a change and holidays should be days of
pleasure, the favorite main dish on feast days is one that
requires more work and greater skill than the faithful spaghetti which needs only plenty of boiling water and a carefully timed period of cooking. *Fettuccine,* not to mention
agnolotti (ravioli, pasta cases), take hours to prepare, and as
time is money (though money hasn't any taste and, according to the Emperor Vespasian, it doesn't smell either) the
cook must allow plenty of time in which to prepare this dish.

* It is impossible to do justice to Trilussa's verses in an English transla-
tion. The above lines are therefore offered merely as a free rendering of
their meaning. [E.A.]

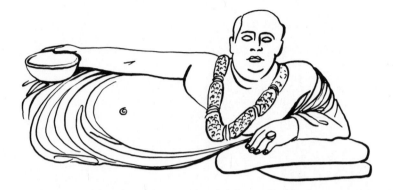

Your guest will be all the more pleased when one of these special "treats" is set before him. If he is afraid of putting on weight, he may comfort himself with the thought that he is in Rome, where Julius Caesar is supposed to have said: "Let me have men about me that are fat!"

FETTUCCINE
Thin Noodles

This recipe for *fettuccine* has the same simplicity that characterizes Roman law. "For every cup of flour, one egg." All the rest is sheer hard work.

3 cups sifted all-purpose flour
3 large eggs
¼ teaspoon salt

Make a hole in middle of flour; put in eggs and salt. Beat eggs with fork, slowly mixing in half the flour. Mix in remaining flour with hands; add a little water if necessary to give the dough the proper consistency for rolling. Let it rest a while. Then roll it out on a floured board until paper thin. Cut

into strips about 7½ to 9½ inches long and ½ inch wide. Set the
fettuccine aside, covered with a towel, for about 2 hours, after
which, following the instructions for ordinary *pastasciutta*,
they are plunged into a large amount of boiling, salted water.
Cookbook writers cannot tell you the exact moment to pour
off the water—this depends on the firmness of the dough, the
amount you use, how far above sea level you live, and the
mood of the gods. All you can do is to taste—and run the
risk of burning your tongue. "But the man who seizes the right
moment is the right man," says Goethe, who had apparently
learned certain basic principles of Roman cookery from
Faustina.

Pasta fatta in casa (homemade noodles) may also be served
quite simply with butter and Parmesan cheese. It deserves
better, however, and in contrast to its simpler sister, *pastasciutta*, it is even served accompanied by both a meat sauce
and ragout. In that case the *fettuccine*, cooked and drained,
are first mixed with sauce and kept warm. At the table, ragout
is added to each plate and generously sprinkled with Parmesan
cheese. For special occasions you may add a piece of butter
the size of a walnut on top of the ragout—more would place
the guest in danger of committing the sin of gluttony.

GNOCCHI
Potato Dumplings or Noodles

Jove, father of the gods, was obliged to vacate his place
on top of the Capitol. His day, *dies Jovis—giovedì,* Thursday—
is, however, something of a red-letter day as is evidenced by
the announcement of *giovedì gnocchi* on the menus of every
restaurant and *osteria* still faithful to tradition. At noon and
in the evening, they serve a dish which the Roman, usually
so mistrustful of the potato (which he accepts only as an
accompaniment to baby lamb), greets with positive enthusiasm.

2½ cups riced or sieved potatoes   1 teaspoon salt
About 1½ cups sifted all-purpose   ¼ teaspoon white pepper
    flour   ½ cup Parmesan cheese
2 egg yolks

Potatoes are carefully kneaded together with flour. Work in
egg yolks, salt, pepper, and cheese. Add more flour if necessary
to handle. Then shape the mixture in cylinders about as thick
as your thumb (about ½ inch). Cut these cylinders in sections
about ⅔ of an inch long. Each section is then pressed flat at
one end with your finger or with a spoon (which is more decorative). Cook one third of the *gnocchi* in 6 quarts of boiling
water and 1½ tablespoons salt—but in this case it is not important to know the right moment to pour off the water. When
the *gnocchi* rise to the surface, they are done. Remove and
keep warm while cooking the rest, one half at a time. Serves
4.

No Roman would ever grant potatoes the honor of being
accompanied by the full line of *sughi.* There are really only
three classic ways to serve *gnocchi*: the most aristocratic is
with brown butter and Parmesan sauce; and the two ordinary
methods are *in bianco* ("in white") with butter and Parmesan

(or *pecorino*) cheese, or with plain meat sauce (see page 56).

At home *gnocchi* are usually served with garnishings: in one dish *gnocchi* will be covered with alternating layers of sauce and Parmesan, at which point the guest should be given the opportunity to sprinkle more Parmesan over his *gnocchi* and thus add to his enjoyment of the feast.

AGNOLOTTI
Filled Pasta Cases (Ravioli)

Like *fettuccine, agnolotti* are a dish with which one may welcome a guest in language more expressive than the language of flowers. To eat *agnolotti* without giving due praise would be unforgivable.

3 cups sifted all-purpose flour	1 teaspoon salt
2 eggs	1 teaspoon butter
1 egg shell full of water	

The dough for *agnolotti* is softer than the dough for *fettuccine* and you can easily shape it into pockets (or squares) to be filled. It is mixed as are *fettuccine*. Knead the dough thoroughly. Then add butter and knead again. Then roll it out with a rolling pin on a floured board.

You must now decide whether to make triangular or quadrangular *agnolotti*. An extremely heretical school of thought even makes round ones. As we are strictly impartial, we shall accept all shapes. The possibilities are as follows:

1. Roll out the dough to the thickness of noodles and cut it into large squares 1½ by 1½ inches or 2 by 2 inches. On each square place a portion of the filling the size of a walnut. The square is then folded diagonally so that it forms a triangle.

2. Roll out the dough somewhat thinner in two separate

layers. Spread the filling on one layer and place the second layer over it. Now cut the two layers through with a knife or even better, with the wheel that is specially made for this purpose, and press the edges of each small square together. This makes four-cornered *agnolotti*.

Cook the *agnolotti* in a large quantity of boiling water, slightly salted, for 7-8 minutes. When they rise to the surface, remove them and drain. Serves 4 to 6.

The most important fillings are:

CON CARNE TRITTATA
With Ground Meat

½ pound boneless pork, veal, or
    lamb
2 tablespoons butter or lard
2 cups spinach
1 slice raw cooked ham

1 egg yolk
½ cup Marsala
⅓ cup grated Parmesan cheese
Salt and pepper
Grated nutmeg

Sauté the pork (veal or lamb are equally good) in butter in a skillet. At the same time cook spinach in a little boiling water. Chop both meat and drained spinach together with a slice of raw ham or put them through the meat grinder (using fine blade). Add the egg yolk, Marsala, cheese, and a little salt, pepper, and nutmeg to taste to give the filling the right consistency and the classic aroma. Serves 4.

CON CARNE E CERVELLO
With Meat and Brains

½ pound lean pork
1 lamb's or pig's brain
1½ tablespoons cooked bone
    marrow
3 egg yolks

Grated nutmeg
½ cup grated Parmesan cheese
Salt
Pepper

Cook the pork and chop it very fine or put it through the meat grinder. Then mash it with either lamb's or pig's brain (which you have cooked quickly in water), bone marrow, egg yolks, a dash of nutmeg, and cheese. Season to taste with salt and a little pepper to complete the filling. Serves 4.

CON SPINACIO E RICOTTA
With Spinach and Ricotta

2 cups spinach
1 pound *ricotta*
¼ cup grated Parmesan cheese

Grated nutmeg
Salt
Pepper

Cook the spinach in a little boiling water and press through a fine sieve. Then press the *ricotta* through the sieve too, and mix both with Parmesan cheese, a dash of nutmeg, and salt and pepper to taste to complete this filling, which is a favorite in Rome.

Ricotta without spinach, but with parsley, Parmesan, nutmeg, salt, and pepper also makes excellent *agnolotti*.

The filled pasta cases are cooked in very hot water and served with a sauce—either with a simple meat sauce, with the juices from a roast, or with fresh, melted brown butter with Parmesan. Serves 4.

GNOCCHI DI SEMOLINA (GNOCCHI ALLA ROMANA)
Semolina (Farina) Dumplings Roman Style

Gnocchi alla Romana are found everywhere on the bill of fare throughout the peninsula, but in Rome they are rare. The proverb about the prophet who is without honor in his own country obviously applies to *gnocchi alla Romana*. "Very unjustly," we hasten to add.

4 cups milk	¼ cup butter
1 cup semolina	2 egg yolks
1 teaspoon salt	¼ teaspoon white pepper
1 cup grated Parmesan cheese	

Make a gruel, such as is prepared wherever there are milk, semolina, and little children. (When the milk is boiling, pour in the semolina and stir vigorously with a wooden spoon about 15 minutes). Instead of serving it with sugar and cinnamon, mix in (after removing from heat) salt, about a fourth of the Parmesan cheese, 2 tablespoons of butter, 2 egg yolks, and pepper. Spread this out on a moistened marble tabletop or a plate (or a plastic work sheet) to about the thickness of a finger. Let it rest 2 hours. Then, with a glass, cut round circles

—or using a knife cut out squares or oblongs as desired—and place the circles (or other shapes) in layers in a fireproof dish, sprinkling each layer generously with Parmesan cheese and dotting the top with beautiful pieces of butter the size of a walnut. The *gnocchi alla Romana* are then baked 15 minutes in the oven (400°F.) or over a charcoal stove where a hot fire, burning steadily under the covered pot, gives the same result. After a quarter of an hour the hot butter will have dropped to the lowest layer, while the top layer will be nicely browned. Serve hot (and preferably in the same dish). Serves 4.

POLENTA
Cornmeal

Among the dishes that replace *pastasciutta* on special occasions, cornmeal stands almost last. As we have said before, Roman cookery shows an inexplicable distrust of foreign carbohydrates. Only on very special occasions—a cold winter's day, for instance—is *polenta,* one of the favorite dishes in Venice, allowed to enter the Roman kitchen. "Beside the quiet hearth in wintertime" one is glad of an excuse to stand three quarters of an hour over the fire.

It is very easy to make *polenta* if you keep in mind three things:

1. You must use a round iron or copper kettle, never an ordinary pot.

2. The cooking time (45 minutes) must be scrupulously checked, for in contrast to making *pastasciutta,* for which no fixed cooking in minutes can be given for the reasons explained previously, a set time is decisive here.

3. *Polenta* must be stirred constantly. This requires a certain

amount of physical strength. In the province of Venetia it is the prerogative of the head of the family to stir. If you use a charcoal stove at least two persons are needed: one to stir the *polenta* and one constantly to tend and fan the fire.

1 cup cornmeal per person
4 cups water
1 teaspoon salt

Sprinkle the *polenta* (cornmeal) slowly into boiling salted water. Stir constantly with a wooden spoon for 45 minutes. After exactly 45 minutes pour the cooked *polenta* out on a smooth marble slab. Cool it and then cut it in slices with a thread or string, not with a knife.

(Note: The *polenta* may be cooked in a heavy saucepan and stirred only occasionally, when a modern range is used. Cover between stirrings. Cut with a stainless knife if desired.)

Heat the slices in a sauce (see pages 51–64) and serve with Parmesan cheese. There are any number of different sauces, but as winter lies in the sign of the pig—from the culinary standpoint—sauces with pork and sausage are the favorites. For example: onions, carrot slices, finely chopped celery and parsley are sautéed in lard (or butter). Then add pork meat, chopped or diced. When the meat has browned, pour a glass of dry white wine over it and allow the wine to boil down. Then add tomato paste and enough water to cover the meat. Continue to simmer the sauce over low heat. Sausages may be added in the last 15 minutes. Salt and pepper are superfluous; instead, a sharp peppercorn and thinly sliced truffles lend the sauce an especially fine flavor. Parmesan cheese, as usual, at the last moment.

Note: the *polenta* slices may also simply be sautéed in oil.

TIMBALLO DI SPAGHETTI (O MACCHERONI)
Spaghetti or Macaroni Timbales

1 pound spaghetti (or macaroni)	Beef juices
⅓ cup butter	Cooked mushrooms, fresh saus-
½ cup grated Parmesan cheese	age, tongue, if desired
12 pitted olives, sliced	Bread crumbs
¾ cup minced cooked ham	2 eggs, well beaten
Mozzarella cheese	

When serving pasta in this form, it is well to use the long tube-shaped macaroni. This time (but only this time) you may break the macaroni into short pieces 3-5 inches long.

Cook them—only 10 minutes—in hot, salted water. Pour off the water and toss the macaroni with butter, Parmesan cheese, olives, and ham. Mozzarella, cut in rounds, and beef juices may be added as desired. Stewed mushrooms, sausage, and bits of tongue also add to the festive mood.

Butter generously a deep round cake pan or casserole (about 8-cup size) and dredge it with bread crumbs. Put ½ of the macaroni mixture into mold. Spread with eggs and place a second layer of macaroni on top. Fill the mold with the macaroni mixture and sprinkle the top with more bread crumbs. Put the *timballo* in a moderately hot oven (375°F.) for about 45 minutes. At the end of that time, take it out of the oven and allow to rest 5 minutes more before unmolding. Serves 4 to 6.

TIMBALLO DI RISO
Rice Timbales

1½ cups rice
3 tablespoons butter
3 tablespoons bone marrow
Meat broth
3 egg yolks
Bread crumbs

For the filling:
6 chicken livers
1 pair lamb's sweetbreads, sliced
1 cup sliced mushrooms
½ pound fresh sausage
Ham, raw or cooked, tongue,
  tomato paste, as desired

Do not wash rice. Sauté it lightly in butter and marrow. (All butter may be used.) Then pour on enough broth to cover the rice, adding more broth if necessary, and cook covered until the rice is almost soft but not too dry. Remove from the heat. Cool and stir in egg yolks, one at a time. Then set the rice aside.

Now prepare a filling by cooking chicken livers, sweetbreads, mushrooms, and sausage together; you may also include diced raw or cooked ham, a small piece of calf's tongue or ox tongue, and a little tomato paste.

When the filling is ready, butter a pudding mold (about 8-cup size) and sprinkle with bread crumbs. Put three quarters of the rice into the mold, make a depression in the center and fill it with the filling you have just made. (The rice surrounds the filling, which does not come in contact with the mold.) Over this put an extra layer (or cover) of rice and sprinkle again with bread crumbs.

Bake the timbale for 1 hour in a medium hot oven (375°F.). When done remove from oven and let it stand 5 minutes before unmolding. Serves 4.

ʊʊ MINESTRE
Soups

There is nothing harder to translate than a culinary term! Perhaps "a one-course dish" would be closer to the Italian, if it did not call up unpleasant memories and spoil your appetite . . . but even so, this does not fully explain the meaning of *le minestre*. Ancient cookbooks speak of *pastasciutta* as *minestra asciutta!* Perhaps it would be more correct to describe the *minestra* as an introduction to the rest of the meal and call it "the first course." When it is so difficult to explain a word from a modern language not one's own, we can appreciate why we have such difficulty understanding those gourmet philosophers, the Deipnosophistai of Athenaeus, who in the year 118 A.D. argued about the current culinary terms in Greek.

"*Pasta o minestra?*—Noodles or vegetable soup?" the waiter in the little *trattoria* asks the guest as he offers him the menu. "*Pasta o minestra?*" ask the children when they come home from school. "*Pasta o minestra?*" the housewife asks herself when she wakes up in the morning and plans the day's meals in the last minutes before she arises. There are arguments enough for both possibilities. *Pastasciutta* is more quickly

80

prepared. Even buying the ingredients for *minestra* takes more time—not to mention the length of time spent in preparing it. Both offer an almost endless number of variations. *Minestra,* however, is more deeply rooted in the history of Rome; the *holuscola pingi lardo uncta* (Horace's garden vegetables provided with plenty of fat) is undoubtedly a description of the ancient form of our present-day *minestra.*

Pastasciutta and *minestra* offer a noteworthy example of coexistence that should make statesmen and politicians pause and think. Nor are the contrasts in this case quite so sharp as they appear to be. There are many *minestre* in which pasta, especially the shorter variety like *rigatoni* and *cannelloni,* are used. Here, too, Parmesan and *pecorino* cheese take up the refrain of the recipe. Making a *minestra,* like preparing a *sugo,* is the art of variation.

In Central Europe a vegetable soup is simply a meat broth in which vegetables are cooked. In Eastern Europe the vegetables are more often cooked in water and the soup finally thickened with a roux. The Roman art of making soup is fundamentally different.

First you chop diced pork rind or bacon with the *odori* (the seasonings) and mix them together. This mixture of fats, fragrant with parsley, basil, and celery, is called a *battuto* (beaten). It is tried out in lard, butter, or olive oil and the result is a *soffritto* (from the Latin, *sub-frigo*—I fry under). Onions and garlic are cooked with it. At the last moment add bay leaves and rosemary.

When the *soffritto* has become liquid in an earthen pot over the blazing fire, add the vegetables and cook them in the fat till tender. When the *soffritto* is thoroughly permeated with all those delicious odors (and not until then) add the water in which, in the last stage, pasta or rice can be boiled down to the desired consistency.

To the Roman, his freedom is his greatest treasure. And

just as none of the Roman tyrants, no matter how hard they tried, was able to destroy his successor, so no man can infringe on the rights of the Roman housewife, on that ancient and sacred practice of varying her cooking at will according to the possibilities of the day.

MINESTRA DI PASTA E BROCCOLI
Vegetable Soup with Pasta and Broccoli

Broccoli, artichokes, and peas are the pride of the vegetable farmer in the Latium region. Broccoli on the menu announces the arrival of autumn. The botanist lists the plant under the varieties of cauliflower, but as mentioned earlier it differs from cauliflower on three points: the flower is firmer, it is not white but light green, and the individual rosettes are definitely more pointed—when they are small they remind one of the seashells on which Neptune's companions on baroque fountains are always trumpeting.

The preparation of vegetable soup with pasta and broccoli can serve as a basic recipe for numerous other combinations.

1 thick slice bacon (or pork rind)	2 cups short pasta
½ garlic clove	Salt
3 sprigs parsley	Pepper
½ onion	Grated Parmesan or *pecorino* cheese
1 tablespoon pork fat	Cooked pig's neck and pieces of ribs, and meat juices if desired
1 tablespoon tomato paste	
1 bunch broccoli	

On a thick slice of bacon or pork rind (or on a slice of fatty smoked ham), using a knife, chop the following aromatic herbs: garlic, parsley, and onion. Put into a heavy soup pot. Dribble pork fat over this from a spoon and when it is all nicely melted, add tomato paste for color. When broccoli are at their best, the season for fresh tomatoes is over. (This does not apply to large cities where the markets carry tomatoes all year round.) Pour 8 cups water on it and toss in the rosettes which you have removed from the broccoli heads. Bring to a boil, simmer, and in half an hour or less they will be almost tender. Then comes the moment for the pasta.

Only an experienced Roman grocer knows the correct names for all types of the "short" pasta . . . but no matter what they are called, they go immediately into this *minestra*. If you haven't any short pasta and cannot get it, you may break the long variety—a deadly sin when preparing spaghetti. The *minestra* is eaten with a spoon. But if this time the preparations are not so strict as the directions for making pasta, you must nevertheless watch carefully for the moment when the pasta becomes soft. At that moment take the *minestra* off the heat. Add salt and pepper to taste. The housewife has nothing more to do but to decide whether to sprinkle the dish with cheese before serving it (the most economical version) or whether to leave it up to the individual to add cheese as he pleases (generous variant). As *minestra* with pasta and broccoli is an autumn dish, let us add that the juice of a ham roast as well as several neck and rib pieces of those pleasant four-footed animals go very well added to this *minestra*. Serves 4 to 6.

MINESTRA DI PASTA E LENTICCHIE, CECI O FAGIOLI
Soup with Pasta and Lentils,
Chick Peas, or Beans

Out of pure respect for pasta we shall mention its name first, but in this recipe pod vegetables, which cook more

slowly, go into the pot first. Of the three vegetables, chick peas hold a special place. These legumes, which are very unjustly neglected north of the Alps, have a special affinity for rosemary, so instead of other herbs only rosemary goes into your *minestra*. This combination of pasta and chick peas in soup is a favorite on Roman menus on Friday. Though historical reasons for this are veiled in darkness, it is known that the Hidalgo with the sad countenance, Don Quixote de la Mancha, was in the habit of eating his chick peas on Fridays too.

Beans also go well with pig's trotters, as well as with bacon rind. And finally lentils have, for very good reason, chosen the bay leaf to accompany them.

Everyone knows that dried pod vegetables should be soaked in water the evening before they are to be used. (In the U.S. this is done only with dried peas, beans, etc.) In Rome the *pizzicagnolo* (proprietor of a small grocery) will soften the chick peas for you.

3 thick slices bacon
1 clove garlic
1 onion
Celery
Parsley
1 carrot
1 cup dried lentils, chick peas, or beans, soaked overnight

1 tablespoon tomato paste or 2 fresh tomatoes
1 cup short pasta
Parmesan cheese
Pig's neck or rib pieces as desired

If the pig's neck or rib pieces are added, you need only a very small amount of bacon. The bacon (or slices of bacon rind) is chopped together with garlic, onion, celery, parsley, and carrot. When Friday is a fast day, the onion and garlic to be used in the *minestra* with pasta and chick peas may be sautéed in a little olive oil.

After the *soffritto* (the fat, fragrant soup foundation) has cooked, add the drained vegetables and pour as much water as needed over them. Simmer vegetables 2 hours or until tender. Add 1 tablespoon of tomato paste or 2 fresh, seeded tomatoes to improve both color and taste. The soup must be so liquid that the pasta which is added at the last moment may swim freely in it. The pasta will also help to thicken the soup. Parmesan cheese is a good addition, but is not absolutely necessary. It is not used with chick peas. Serves 4 to 6.

MINESTRA DI RISO E FAGIOLI   (PISELLI)
Soup with Rice and Beans (or Peas)

As already mentioned, rice does not play an important part in Roman cookery. It appears occasionally in a *minestra* made with dried lentils, beans, or peas—and to prove how unjust the Roman's mistrust of it is, pasta may be served one day in the *minestra* and, for a change, the next day *minestra* may be served with rice in place of the pasta, following the preceding recipe in other respects.

Pick over and clean the rice, but do not wash it. Cook it exactly 18 minutes before serving—one minute more or less would be a mistake.* Perhaps that is why the Roman, who depends more on providence, intuition and omnipresent chance than on the relentless clock, cannot really come to terms with rice.

* This applies to Italian rice, which may be purchased in Italian grocery stores. For "converted" and partially precooked rice, follow directions on the package. They will not give the same result in these recipes as the whole Italian rice.

MINESTRA DI RISO E INDIVIA (CICORIA)
Soup with Rice and Endive (Chicory)

The somewhat bitter endive is often served as salad, especially as the Romans like to eat a salad with their beef-steak. In other parts of Italy endive is considered much too bitter. Anyone who has learned to cook rice properly can make an excellent *minestra* with rice and endive.

2 thick slices bacon	1 tablespoon fat
1 clove garlic	1 pound endive
3 sprigs parsley	Water or meat broth
1 stalk celery	1 cup rice

Chop the bacon very fine with a little garlic, parsley, and celery and sauté in fat. Add the cleaned endive, and cover with water or meat broth. When the endive is almost tender, add the rice, which must cook 18 minutes more. Add more liquid if necessary. It is perhaps not superfluous to repeat that rice south of the Alps is picked over by hand and freed of all impurities, but that it is *not* washed in cold water any more than is cornmeal. Serves 4.

BRODO
Meat Broth

Meat broth is one of the few dependable international institutions. The French persist in cooking their *pot au feu* in an earthen pot which they seal by putting a strip of moist dough between the lid and the pot, and they cook it for at least 6 hours. Naturally they turn out an essentially better soup than their impatient neighbors. No matter where soup is simmered the indispensable ingredients are a huge piece of meat (beef), marrow bone, carrots, celery, parsley (stems and leaves). Little boxes filled with cubes made of salt, monosodium glutamate, caramel, and suet, cannot quite replace the old dish even when they have a picture of an ox on the cover.

The superiority of meat broth is not unknown in Rome, but as fattened oxen are rare in the Apennines, it appears on the table only on special occasions. Even then it is sometimes made of beef and lamb combined, and it is usually served with garnishings, for example *cappelletti,* or "little hats." Whether they really look like little hats depends upon the prevailing mode.

CAPPELLETTI IN BRODO   (TORTELLINI)
Little Hats in Soup (Tartlets)

Noodle dough
1 slice of raw ham
1 slice of *mortadella*
1 pork chop, boned
1 cooked chicken or turkey
   breast
1 calf's brain

1 egg
1 teaspoon salt
⅛ teaspoon pepper
⅛ teaspoon grated nutmeg
½ cup Marsala wine
¼ cup Parmesan cheese
Clear meat broth

The dough for the *cappelletti* is the same as noodle dough (see fettuccine, pages 69–70) but it should be about ⅙ of an inch thick when rolled out. Take a small glass (or biscuit cutter) and cut out round pieces, about 2 inches in diameter, from this dough. Now make the following filling:

Chop or put through the grinder the raw ham, *mortadella,* pork, chicken or turkey, and brain. To this meat add egg and salt, pepper, nutmeg, Marsala wine (wine from the Western corner of Sicily, somewhat like Malaga and Madeira), and cheese. In the center of each round of dough place a bit of this filling (about the size of a hazel nut or a walnut), fold the dough in half carefully, and close it by pressing the sides together. When the filling is laid on the dough in the shape of a ring the result is little hats of a different form. Allow 10-15 *cappelletti* per person. Twenty minutes before the meal strain the meat broth and place the *cappelletti* gently in enough clear broth to cover them. Simmer till tender. A little grated Parmesan goes very well with this dish.

SEMOLINO IN BRODO
Semolina or Grits in Broth

Ten minutes before serving stir the grits slowly into the strained and boiling broth. Use 2 tablespoons grits for each 4 cups of meat broth. The soup must be liquid. Grated Parmesan is stirred in at the last moment when the grits are already soft. Each 4 cups broth will serve 3 well.

STRACCIATELLA
Egg-ribbon Soup

6 cups meat broth
3 eggs
3 tablespoons flour or finely
   ground grits

3 tablespoons grated Parmesan
cheese

When the broth is cooked and strained, take out a ladleful and allow to cool. Meanwhile in a deep tureen mix eggs, flour or grits, and Parmesan cheese. (The addition of a little grated nutmeg is permitted, but is not absolutely necessary.) All this is then stirred well and mixed with the ladleful of soup, which has cooled by this time. Now, stirring constantly, pour the contents of the tureen slowly into the boiling broth, so that it sets and forms longish ribbons or strips (*stracci*). Serves 4.

ꝯꝯ PIETANZE
Dishes for the
Second Course

Pietanze is a hard word to translate. When a bill of fare offers *"minestra-pietanza-dolce,"* neither linguists nor culinary experts know whether *pietanza* means a meat, fish, or a vegetable dish—or whether *dolce* (dessert) is some sort of a starchy dish, an ice cream, or a fruit compote. We cannot go wrong if we call *pietanza* the second course.

Here, however, we must avoid a misunderstanding. In Central Europe and America the first course, soup, is merely a promise that will be redeemed in the second course; the focal point of the meal is the meat dish, with which, according to the season of the year, personal taste, or geographical latitude, potatoes, dumplings, noodles, or rice are served, accompanied by vegetables or salad—whereas the Romans, both ancient and modern, apportion things quite differently. *Pastasciutta* or *minestra* is intended to satisfy one's hunger (except on special feast days when the three soups described last in the preceding chapter appear). Whatever comes next is merely a welcome addition. The midday meal for most of the inhabitants of the Eternal City is sure to be one of the dishes we have already described, especially if bread accompanies the *pastasciutta*. When, in addition, there is a glass or even half a quart of

90

Frascati, Marino, Albano, or Grottaferrata, and if this is followed by strong black coffee, it is truly an excellent meal.

Here the stranger who wishes to learn about ancient Rome, the Rome of the Middle Ages, and modern Rome, and at the same time enjoy Roman cookery, runs into difficulties; he finds that he can scarcely eat all of his *fettuccine* and is disappointed when he sees so much of the plate around his beefsteak.

"I thought it would be different," he says. "Much more Lucullan. Then what do princes and high prelates eat?"

"The same as we other Romans," is the only correct answer. *Pastasciutta* and *minestra* reach even to the cardinals.

Between the Roman aristocrat and the people of Rome there is scarcely any difference either in language or style of living. The palaces in which princely families live for five hundred years shelter families of servants and cooks who spend about the same length of time under the same roof as the owners. It would be a miracle if they had not become like each other —though miracles are much more frequent in Rome than anywhere else.

The patrician in ancient Rome called his slaves "the family." All dignitaries in the Vatican, from the Master of Ceremonies to the recruit in the Swiss Guards, are part of the *familia pontificia*. The great families of the "Black Aristocracy" have had many centuries in which to draw this sort of "family" closer together—and even the aristocrats who stem from the canteen followers of the Napoleonic army have now had a century and a half to become accustomed to the ways of Rome.

Aristocrats and servants both speak good Roman. But of the two million inhabitants in the city, too many come from other provinces; they are descendants of the noble Red Shirts, or the wretched Black Shirts, and too foreign to be able to compete with the real Romans. The language of Rome is per-

haps not altogether unknown to the movie fan: Aldo Fabrizi and Anna Magnani speak it perfectly. The twitterings of curvaceous princesses from the provinces are a very different thing. It is still spoken correctly in Roman palaces and upper-class houses around the Piazza Navona, the Campo di Fiori, and in Trastevere, the old streets on the right bank of the Tiber. There, too, the citadels of Roman cookery, with their *fornelli* (charcoal stoves) and their *cocci* (earthen pots), still resist the onrush of our century of mediocre uniformity. The castle-like structures, which were built with stones from the Colosseum and from ruined temples, preserve traditions which in the modern houses in the higher section of the city, the *quartieri alti,* lose all meaning. One of these traditions is the very special relation between the so-called "upper classes" and the "lower classes." The latter long ago lost the servility which marked the attitude of the peasants and citizens of Eastern Europe toward their "lords," and the lords have learned to respect their servants as human beings. In Rome innumerable misunderstandings and antagonisms are eliminated: everyone eats out of the same pot.

ᘛᘚ PIATTI DI CARNE
Meat Dishes

L'ABBACCHIO
Lamb

On the golden background of the oldest basilica niches in Rome, lambs and sheep, symbols of the faithful, graze. Saints pray to the lamb, the lamb of God.

On the slopes of the Apennines, on the hills between sea and mountains, on the promontory of the enchantress Circe, on the grassy expanse of the Campagna, sheep graze and lambs gambol. They graze and grow fat for the Romans.

When, on a quiet Sunday at home, the Roman thinks of the one thing that compensates for a week of toil and trouble, he thinks first of the little lamb that comes out of the oven—*abbacchio arrosto* (roast baby lamb). What roast beef is to the Englishman and roast chicken to the citizen of the former Hapsburg monarchy—a symbol of solid prosperity—so is his lamb to the *civis Romanus*. When the oven door is opened and the crisp brown lamb appears, one can be sure that the

doors of the Janus Temple are closed—peace reigns in the world.

ABBACCHIO (AGNELLO) ARROSTO
Roast Milk-fed Baby Lamb

1 whole baby lamb (or kid)
Oil or lard
Salt
Pepper
Garlic

Potatoes
Raisins
Rosemary leaves
Olive oil

The housewife who has only a wood or charcoal stove—and there are many—prepares the uncooked lamb and takes it to the baker. The *fornari* (bakers) are masters of their art: one glance at the lamb (or kid) is enough to tell them whether it will be done in three quarters of an hour or in an hour. They take the round (or long) pans out of the oven exactly on the minute, just as the artist at preparing *pastasciutta* knows exactly the right second to pour off the water. The housewife's work is therefore confined to cleaning the lamb, rubbing it with oil (or lard), salt and pepper, and inserting half a clove of garlic (sliced) in several places. As potatoes, cut in quarters, take exactly the same time to cook as baby lamb, they are placed in layers in the baking pan with the lamb, sprinkled with salt, raisins and rosemary leaves, and dotted generously with olive oil. Roast in moderate oven 350°F. about 1 hour or until lamb is cooked to desired doneness. Potatoes will also be done.

A crisp green salad transforms this Sunday dish into a feast.

COSCETTO DI AGNELLO ARROSTO
Roast Leg of Lamb

Instead of the whole lamb a fore or hind leg provides an excellent meal, especially when it is well larded.

1 leg or shoulder of lamb (either fore or hind leg, 5 to 6 pounds)	½ teaspoon pepper
	1 clove garlic, minced
Bacon or pieces of ham (about ¼ pound)	16 medium potatoes
	2 tablespoons oil
1½ teaspoons salt	1 teaspoon rosemary leaves
1 teaspoon marjoram leaves	

To lard the lamb take pieces of bacon, or cut in strips, lengthwise, 1 to 2 inch-long pieces of raw ham "from the mountains," preferably from Norcia, which has the best pork butchers. The pieces to be used for larding are rolled in salt, marjoram, pepper, and finally in garlic. Insert them in slits cut in the flesh in 10 to 15 places. Slice the potatoes and season them with oil and rosemary, put them in the pan with the leg of lamb. Roast in preheated oven at 300°F., 30-35 minutes to the pound (to suit the American taste, 20 minutes to the pound if you follow the European way). If roasted over a wood fire, the result will be incomparable. Serves 8.

ABBACCHIO BRODETTATO
Braised Lamb

The word *brodettato* comes from the good old days (the old days were always good) when the Easter soup (*brodo*—meat broth), with the yolks of Easter eggs that had been sprinkled with lemon juice and marjoram, came on the table —exactly like this dish, which is really not a soup at all.

2¼ pounds boneless lamb or kid	Pepper
¼ pound lean or fat smoked ham	3 egg yolks, beaten
2 onions, sliced	Juice of 1 lemon
Flour	Parsley
½ cup Frascati or Orvieto (or any dry white wine)	½ teaspoon marjoram

The lamb (or kid) is diced or cut in pieces lengthwise and cooked with ham and onion slices. Dredge the meat with flour (this is never done in Roman dishes otherwise) and when even the flour is browned, add a glass of dry white Frascati or Orvieto wine. These may be purchased in some liquor stores in the United States, but if not available, use any dry white wine. When the wine is absorbed, cover the pieces of meat with water, add plenty of pepper, and simmer over low heat till tender.

When the meat is tender and the juice thick, beat together three egg yolks with the lemon juice, a little parsley and marjoram. A few minutes before serving, slowly add the egg mixture to the juice and meat, which has been kept warm, but do not allow to boil or the eggs will curdle. The sauce must be smooth and yellow. Serves 4.

CORATELLA DI ABBACCHIO BRODETTATO
Lamb's Heart, Lungs, Liver in Broth

Coratella are the heart, lungs, and liver, which are often bought along with the diaphragm and the stomach.

1 young lamb's heart, lungs, and liver	2 teaspoons salt
3 tablespoons fat	½ teaspoon pepper
1 onion, chopped	3 egg yolks, beaten
1 cup dry white wine (Frascati or Orvieto)	3 tablespoons chopped parsley
	1 teaspoon marjoram leaves
	2 lemons

First separate heart, lungs, and liver. Dice them or cut them up lengthwise. Sauté the lungs in fat, then add onion, and when it has taken on a beautiful color, pour ½ cup wine over it and allow it to cook gently. Twenty minutes later add the heart and ¼ cup of wine and a quarter of an hour after that the liver and ¼ cup wine. If the wine is too quickly absorbed more may be added (but thinned with water). Add salt and pepper. When the sauce has thickened and the heart and lungs are tender, add the beaten egg yolks with parsley, marjoram, and juice of 1 lemon and simmer as in the preceding recipe. Do not allow it to boil. Garnish with lemon wedges. Serves 4 to 6.

ANIMELLE D'ABBACCHIO
Lamb Sweetbreads

1 pound lamb's sweetbreads	¼ teaspoon salt
1 onion, chopped	⅛ teaspoon pepper
½ cup raw ham or lean bacon, slivered	Butter
	Broth or wine

Wash the lamb's white sweetbreads in lukewarm water to free them of blood and cook very briefly in a little water to firm them so the tissue can be removed easily. Mix onion, ham or bacon, salt and pepper. Cook with the sweetbreads in a little butter. Then simmer them in water (or broth or wine thinned with water) for three quarters of an hour. When done remove the sweetbreads to a hot platter, add a piece of butter to the liquid in which they have cooked, and pour over the sweetbreads. Serves 4.

ABBACCHIO ALLA CACCIATORA
Baby Lamb Hunter's Style

2½ pounds of boneless baby lamb	1 rosemary branch
2 tablespoons fat	Sage leaves
Salt	2 tablespoons all-purpose flour
Pepper	White wine or vinegar
1 clove of garlic, minced	2 anchovies

The originality of this method of cooking lamb lies in the unusual combination of seasonings—anchovies and sage. Strange as it may seem, the result proves that it is worth the effort.

Dice the meat or cut in long, thin strips, and brown it in fat. Salt it and pepper it. When it is a beautiful brown add garlic, rosemary, and a few sage leaves. Let this cook a few minutes, then sprinkle the pieces of meat with flour, and when the flour is nicely brown pour white wine (or vinegar thinned with water) over it. Now cook for an hour over medium heat, adding water from time to time if necessary.

Before serving, spoon out a little of the juice to which you add anchovies; add this to the rest of the juice and pour it all back over the meat. As the anchovies are fairly salty, take care to salt the meat very lightly in the beginning. Serves 4 to 5.

TESTA DI ABBACCHIO
Sheeps' Head

There are sheeps' heads everywhere. In Rome they are especially prized as their brain is a delicacy. Brainless and carefully scrubbed, they can then be roasted in the oven.

1 sheep's head	Salt
Parsley	Pepper
Capers	Butter
Lemon juice	

The brain can be served as a *fritto* (see page 30) or it can be chopped, sprinkled with parsley and capers, and generously moistened with lemon juice. Salt and pepper it and sauté it in butter. When it is done, at the last moment pour the remaining brown butter over it.

The rest of the head (after removing eyes and ears) can be brushed with fat and sprinkled with salt and pepper; broiled or grilled in the oven it yields so much meat that there is enough to keep a piece of bread, *una pagnotta,* from seeming too dry.

BRACIOLINI DI AGNELLO
Lamb Cutlets

Lamb cutlets are smaller, tenderer, and certainly just as tasty as pork cutlets.

3-4 small lamb cutlets per person	Parsley
1 slice of bacon per person	1 celery stalk
1 clove of garlic	Fat
1 small onion	Salt and pepper
Marjoram	Tomato paste

Have your butcher pound the cutlets very thin. On each strip of bacon place a garlic clove, an onion, a bit of marjoram, a sprig of parsley, and a celery stalk. Chop very fine, as in *minestra,* and sauté in fat. Sauté the cutlets in the same fat till brown; salt and pepper them. Add a little tomato paste thinned with water and cook till tender. Serve the cutlets with salad, artichokes, or peas according to the season of the year.

BRACIOLINI DI AGNELLO AI FERRI
Lamb Cutlets Grilled (or Broiled)

Anyone fortunate enough to have a wood fire cannot make a mistake with these lamb cutlets. Lamb cutlets that have been pounded thin, sprinkled with salt and pepper, and brushed carefully with oil are easily roasted on the spit to a crisp brown in a few minutes.

The fire must not be too hot and the cutlets must be very

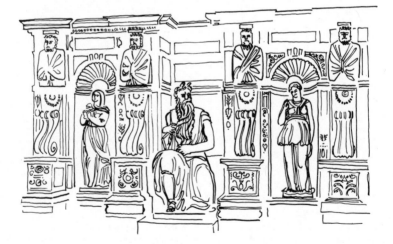

lightly brushed with oil or fat. Too much fat would drip into the fire and cause it to smoke and give off an unpleasant odor. Serve the cutlets with an extra piece of butter the size of a walnut.

MANZO
Beef

BISTECCA
Beefsteak

The finest cattle pasture in Tuscany—far from Rome. No wonder the Roman enjoys a Florentine fillet of beef, washed down with a glass of red wine from Machiavelli's old vineyard (that shrewed political theoretician smiles slyly from the label to see how little his work has aged even today). To be sure Rome is *caput mundi*, leader of the world, but in many respects the city on the Arno surpasses it. For example, the popes had to call on a Florentine artist to decorate the Sistine Chapel—a certain Michelangelo Buonarroti.

Patriotic Romans at the cook stove do not agree. "The Tuscans," they say, "keep the finest pieces, the ones God intended for beefsteak, for themselves." There is something in this theory. The Tuscans are descended from the Etruscans, whom the Romans robbed of their dominion over the peninsula; they have no intention of losing their dominion over beefsteak too. Nevertheless it is hard to keep up with them. Perhaps one might try the following:

Take a well-fed ox in the bloom of its prime, cut out the piece of the loin in such a way that the round contrafilet (scientifically, the *psoas major*) alongside the rump lies opposite the crosscut of the *erector trunci*. It would be a complicated procedure. Let us say more simply: "Go to a butcher you can trust and buy beefsteak 1¼ to 2¼ inches thick. Leave it on ice three or four days (or longer)."

Then put the steak on a gridiron over the charcoal fire, after the fire has been burning for some time and the flame is steady and does not smoke or have to be fanned, which would cause the ashes to fly out. The expert reckons the length of time for grilling by the age of the ox, the temperature of the heat, the thickness of the steak, and the eagerness of the man who has ordered it. The cook is strictly forbidden to pierce the meat with a fork, as this causes loss of valuable juices. He may use a spoon to turn it, but in that case he must have sensory nerves at the very tip of the spoon. When the steak is done, put it on a warm platter, brush it with oil or a piece of butter into which you have worked a little parsley. Pepper may be added as desired. When the *bistecca*—which is always spoken of as *bella*, beautiful (just as pasta is always called *buona*, good)—is accompanied by a noble wine of Latium, red wine from Olivano, Palestrina, or Zagarolo, or the strong Barbera d'Agnani, that is indeed a red-letter day, worthy of being marked by a little white stone—*albo signari lapillo*—as the old Romans did when they made a calendar by counting pebbles.

UMIDO
Braising

Italians prefer meat without juice. The juice—*il sugo del umido*—is served at the same time, but in a separate bowl, though generally it remains in the kitchen waiting to play a guest role. It is indispensable in making *supplì* and is used in

various meat sauces to be served with *pastasciutta*. A Sunday *umido* solves many problems at the beginning of the week.

4 pounds beef for roasting	1 onion
½ cup bacon or ham pieces	Celery
Salt	Carrots
Pepper	Sage
Marjoram	Basil
Garlic	½ cup of strong red wine
Parsley	2 tablespoons tomato paste
Lard	

For the *umido* the Romans use the cut of meat that in other countries is used for roast beef. To begin with it is highly seasoned; the bacon or ham pieces are dipped in salt, pepper, marjoram, and crushed garlic. In the pot put the classic foundation of the *minestra:* the pieces of bacon that have been well worked together with garlic and parsley and tried out in lard. Then add a mixture of finely chopped onion, celery, carrots (as desired), also sage and basil. Sauté the vegetables lightly with the herbs, add a little water, and cook till tender. (Or just add a small amount of water without sautéing and cook till tender.) Before adding the meat to the pot, tie it carefully so that it will hold its shape. Then brown the meat in the pot with the cooked down ingredients, and pour wine over it. The red wines from Grottaferrata and Velletri are especially good for this. When the wine is absorbed, add the tomato paste, which gives both extra flavor to the sauce and a rich, dark red color. The *umido* is then covered and simmered till tender for about 2½ hours over medium heat. Watch carefully, and when the water is absorbed add the necessary amount of water.

LO STUFATINO
Boiled Beef

The *stufatino* differs from the *umido* in two essential points: the meat is first cut in slices, then laid in the pot; and the sauce is much more liquid, so that vegetables (generally celery stalks) may be cooked in it. The ideal cut for this would be the fillet, but as this noble portion of the ox seldom comes to Rome, the other lean cuts may appear in its stead.

1 onion, sliced	Salt
1½ tablespoons lard	Pepper
4 slices bacon, chopped	½ teaspoon marjoram
1 clove garlic	¾ cup red wine
2 pounds boneless lean beef, sliced or cubed	2 tablespoons tomato paste or several fresh tomatoes

Sauté a sliced onion in lard, then add bacon which has been mixed with garlic, and finally add the meat, which you have sprinkled with salt, pepper, and marjoram. Pour red wine over it. When the wine is absorbed, add tomato paste or several seeded and peeled tomatoes. Add water to cover and cook until the meat is tender. Keep adding water if necessary. The juice must be dark red (a sort of Rembrandt color) and liquid. It can also be used for various sauces and often is used to give a special note to tripe. Serves 4.

INVOLTINI DI MANZO
Beef Rolls (Rolled Beef)

The *involtini* appear in their various shapes when it is important to make a marvelous dish out of a small amount of meat. Whereas a thin slice of meat looks like nothing but a thin slice of meat, rolled around a slice of bacon it is decidedly more appetizing. For *mundus vult decipi*, says the proverb: the world likes to be deceived. "Deceive or be deceived," Nestroy declares, "there is no other way, and the man who thinks there is, is deceiving himself." The various *involtini*, however, are a specially delicious deception; we shall therefore give two versions here and a third, saltimbocca, on pages 116–117 in the section on veal.

1½ pounds lean boneless beef	White bread
Roast pork, chicken, bacon and	Milk
ham	1 or 2 egg yolks
Garlic	Parmesan cheese
Marjoram	Lard or oil
Salt	Marsala wine
Pepper	Tomato paste
Nutmeg	

Cut beef in long strips about 4 inches long by 2 inches wide. Pound it thin and prepare the following stuffing:

Mix together chopped leftover roast pork or chicken, smoked ham and bacon with a small amount of garlic and marjoram. Salt and pepper it to taste and sprinkle it with grated nutmeg. Then add an equal amount of white bread which you have softened in milk, 1 or 2 egg yolks, and some grated Parmesan cheese. Put some of this mixture on each slice of meat. Wrap the slices of meat around the stuffing, tie with thread or fasten with toothpicks, and place in a flat earthenware dish with lard or oil. Brown the *involtini,* scrape the bottom of the pan, pour a little Marsala wine over them, and when this has evaporated, pour in water or tomato paste that has been greatly thinned, with water to cover, and simmer gently, covered, till tender. Serves 4.

UCCELLETTI DI CAMPAGNA
Little Birds from the Country

1½ pounds lean boneless beef	Sage
Salt	White bread
Pepper	Bacon
Smoked ham	Oil or fat

As in the preceding recipe, cut the meat in strips, pound it thin, salt and pepper it, and wrap it around a piece of fat smoked ham on which you have placed a sage leaf (or a little dried sage). Now put the *involtini* on a spit or skewers so that each slice of meat is followed by a square piece of white bread and a piece of bacon. Brush with oil or fat. The *rosticcieri*—owners of fried-food stores—follow tradition and roast the little "birds" over the charcoal fire, paying close attention that the heat is on both sides of the spit and not only underneath it, so that the fat drips off without smoking. The owner of a modern broiler should lay the spit or skewers on the broiling pan and broil under moderate heat till done, turning several times. Serves 4.

CODA ALLA VACCINARA
Oxtail Dairymaid Style

If it is true that the Tuscans keep the best pieces of beef for themselves, it is equally true that the Romans are expert at making excellent dishes out of the despised portions: tail, stomach, liver, kidneys, and—*horribile dictu*—even out of the ox's guts.

1 oxtail	3 tablespoons fat
Ox cheeks	Salt
2 slices bacon	Pepper
2 onions	½ cup dry red wine
1 clove garlic	3 tablespoons tomato paste
5 sprigs parsley	1 bunch celery
1 carrot	

Cut the oxtail in rounds. To give the juice the right thickness, cut the same quantity of ox cheeks into pieces. As for *minestra*, chop bacon with onions, garlic, parsley, and carrot, sauté in fat, and set the oxtail and cheeks on it. When the meat has browned, salt and pepper it and pour wine over it. Let the wine reduce a little, cover the whole with tomato paste which you have thinned with water, and then pour in as much water as needed to cover; cover pot. If this is ready to start cooking at seven o'clock in the morning, it will be done in time for the midday meal at one o'clock. Serves 4 to 8 depending on size of oxtail.

Cooked celery is traditional with oxtail. If you plan to serve celery, soak the celery stalks at noon in hot water and at half past twelve add them to the oxtail. This dish is worth the long period of cooking.

TRIPPA
Tripe (Calf's or Cow's Stomach)

To prepare tripe takes almost as long as to prepare oxtail —but it would be difficult to spend a Saturday morning more profitably. Anyone who has other business at this time must eat his Saturday meal in a *trattoria* where the bulletin board announces that the choice dish awaits him in great iron kettles. In buying tripe be sure that at least half of it consists of the small part of the calf's stomach, which is considered a special delicacy. (Tripe may be purchased precooked in some markets.)

Uncooked calf's or cow's stomach (about 2 pounds)	Meat juices
	Parmesan cheese
1 carrot	1 peppermint leaf
1 onion	Salt
2 stalks celery	Pepper
6 sprigs parsley	

As with soup meat, the stomach must cook covered fully 6 hours, with carrot, onion, celery, and parsley added. When tender, cut tripe in long strips about 2 inches wide and simmer them another half hour in the juice of the *umido* (or *stufatino*). When the tripe is thoroughly saturated with the juice, it is done. Serves 4.

Whereas with *pastasciutta* the guest has only two possibilities to choose from—grated *pecorino* or Parmesan—here he has a third choice: Parmesan to which a minced peppermint leaf has been added (and since by decision of the Council of Trent the will of man is free, he must make his own choice here in full awareness of his responsibility). Add salt and pepper as desired.

FEGATO
Liver

6 onions, sliced	Salt
¼ cup olive oil or fat	Pepper
1½ pounds liver, sliced thinly	Several bay leaves

Slice the onions in rings and sauté them lightly in olive oil (other fats are not used so frequently). Remove membrane from liver and add to onions. Add salt, pepper to taste and a few bay leaves. Cook quickly over a hot fire in a few minutes. Serves 4.

PAGLIATA
Ox Gut

It seems strange to use ox gut for gastronomical purposes. We grant this part of the ox's anatomy the ability to touch our hearts only in the form of violin strings. But when one realizes that Bach's Sixth Sonata for the violoncello is played in part on the ox's large intestine, we can forgive the Roman for gazing with pleasure on his *pagliata,* whether it is served with rice or (as happens more frequently) with a special form of short pasta known as *rigatoni.*

Ox gut	Salt
Bacon	Pepper
Garlic	Red wine
Celery	Tomato paste
Parsley	Rigatoni or rice
Fat	*Pecorino* or Parmesan cheese

As soon as possible after purchasing, remove the skin from the intestine, cut the gut in pieces about 7½ inches long, and tie them in circles. Chop the bacon with garlic, celery, and parsley, try it out in hot fat, add the rings, and brown, stirring constantly. Add salt and pepper and pour red wine over all. When the wine has evaporated, add water in which you have put a few spoonfuls of tomato paste (or tomato purée). Cook from 3 to 4 hours, adding wine or water as necessary. The rings should have shrunk and be tender. Now lay the rings on the *rigatoni* which you have cooked, or the rice which has cooked fully 18 minutes (if you use Italian rice), and sprinkle with *pecorino* or Parmesan cheese.

ROGNONI IN UMIDO
Braised Kidneys

2 veal kidneys	Salt
Butter or oil	Pepper
Red wine	Paprika
2 cups chopped onions	Parsley
2 fresh tomatoes	

To free the kidneys properly of any liquid, cut them in thin slices, soak them in boiling water until red color is gone, drain thoroughly, and sauté them quickly over high heat (5 minutes) in a little butter or oil. Then put them in a sieve to drain. They will be dry in 15 minutes. Marinate in red wine. Meanwhile sauté onions in butter until soft and golden, add tomatoes, peeled and seeded, and when they have cooked down sufficiently, add the slices of kidney. Add salt, pepper, and paprika to taste, and again pour red wine over them. (White, dry Frascati may also be used for this purpose.) Cover and simmer over low heat about 10 minutes or till done. Before serving add a sprinkling of parsley.

POLPETTE (COPPIETTE) DI MANZO
Meat Balls of Beef

Chopped or minced (ground) meat, mixed with softened white bread and an egg and fried in fat, is probably the most international of all dishes in our tediously uniform world. The Swedes mix beef, lamb, and pork meat together and serve it with a cream sauce. The Americans love the large shape and swear by their hamburgers. Roman meat balls (*polpette*) differ from their distant relatives as follows:

1. In the meat-bread mixture put a generous helping of Parmesan cheese, several raisins, and pine nuts (*pignoli*). Pine nuts may be purchased in Italian grocery stores.

2. The finished meat balls are served in the juice of the *umido* (see pages 102–104).

Whereas everywhere else except in America the remains of the roast and of soup meat are commonly used in the local chopped-meat preparation, in Rome, as in the United States, fresh, raw meat is used.

MAIALE–PORCO
Pork

Horace describes himself as a little pig from the herd of Epicurus, *Epicuri de grege porcus,* which proves that the nourishing four-footer was by no means despised in ancient days. The modern citizen too has a tender regard for the animal, whose ribs, legs, neck, and tail (the *spuntature*) give that special flavor to the *minestra.* And never would a modern Roman begin the New Year without a pig's foot.

Pork comes from a long way off—from Modena, where the great pig's knuckle, *lo zampone,* is skillfully prepared and heavily salted, to the delight of regions less generously blessed with pigs. Only since the end of World War II has Santa Claus been considered the symbol of the blessed, joyous season of the Saturnalia, but the pigs' knuckles hanging in the shops of the *pizzicagnoli* (small groceries), and *cotechini* (sausages) stuffed with pork fat are early signs of the coming change in the year.

Pigs' knuckles are first soaked in running water to free them of salt; the *cotechino* is cooked in water just as it is, the cooking varying according to the size, from 3½ to 4 hours. Lentils, always served with this dish, guarantee a sound financial situation in the new year (if it doesn't work, repeat the dose in a year).

FEGATELLI
Liver Slices

A recipe that has not changed for two thousand years.

1½ pounds liver	Bay leaves
Pepper	White bread
Salt	Fat or butter

Cut the liver in pieces as long as your thumb and twice as thick. Pepper and salt them. Then cover the surface with bay leaves, wrap up each piece in a bit of the pig's large caul, if you have it, and secure it with two or three toothpicks. Put the pieces on a spit (or on a skewer) and cook over the open fire, inserting between each piece of liver a piece of white bread that has been dipped in fat or butter. Lacking a spit, the liver slices may be fried in an iron skillet with a very small amount of fat. The melted caul is fat enough. Serves 4.

PORCHETTA
Roast Pork

2 cloves garlic, sliced	Salt
6 peppermint leaves	Pepper
1 teaspoon fennel seeds	½ cup dry white wine
1 tablespoon olive oil	4 pounds boned loin of pork

In a flat earthen pot (if you haven't a flameproof one, use a Dutch oven or large heavy skillet) sauté garlic, peppermint leaves, and fennel seeds in oil. Salt and pepper them and pour wine over them. When the wine has evaporated, put in the pork. Cover and cook slowly about 1¾ hours or until meat is tender. Serves 5 to 6.

For important feast days like the *Festa di Noiantri* (the special festival of the Trastevere section of the city on the right bank of the Tiber), the roast pork takes the form of a whole suckling pig. The delightful little animal is seasoned with every known herb. Cooked whole and lying beside a mound of rolls (round *pagnotte*, long *sfilatini*, or the eel-shaped *ciriole*), it awaits the customer who chooses a roll and fills it with a piece of the succulent meat. From there the people of Trastevere go on to the *osteria,* where they will drink abundantly of the three classic kinds of Frascati wine, *asciutto* (dry), *sulla vena* (medium sweet) and *cannellino* (sweet).

LOMBELLO DI MAIALE
Pork Fillet

Marcus Gavius Apicius calls pork fillets *Lumbuli.* In Latin grammars the word is not given with the *plurale tantum* of the second declension. In Italian this cut of pork is usually called *filetto.* Today the old word exists only within the walls of Rome.

Pork fillet	White bread
Salt	Raw Ham
Pepper	Bay leaves

In Rome large cubes of pork fillet are sprinkled with salt and pepper, and run on the spit or skewers with large slivers of white bread strung between the pieces of meat, which are covered on one side with a piece of raw ham (prosciutto) and on the other with a bay leaf. The meat is then cooked over the charcoal fire, leaving a groove between the coals into which the fat drips—not into the fire. If you do not have a charcoal stove and must use modern equipment, lay the skewers on a broiling pan and bake in the oven at 350°F. until done, or place under moderate heat in the broiler, turning often. The pork must be well done with no pinkness. Season to taste with salt and pepper. 1½ pounds pork fillet will serve 4.

VITELLO
Veal

Veal is not among the commoner meats on the Roman menu. . . . Restaurants offer veal cutlets to show that they can keep up with international competition even in this field. On one point they are definitely successful: veal cooked with Marsala wine is equally as good as veal in Madeira sauce. In the centuries-old stone vaults on the western tip of Sicily, a wine (Marsala) ripens that can ennoble roast pork or roast lamb and is absolutely indispensable for veal, which tends to be somewhat insipid.

SCALOPPINE DI VITELLO AL MARSALA
Veal Cutlets with Marsala

1½ pounds veal cutlet, sliced thin, Italian style	2 tablespoons all-purpose flour
	2 tablespoons butter
Salt	½ cup Marsala
Pepper	Broth or water

Pound the cutlets very thin, salt and pepper them, and cut into 8 pieces. Dip in flour and sauté in hot butter. When they are beautifully brown, pour Marsala over them. Before the wine has entirely evaporated, thin the sauce with a little broth or water. Serves 4.

INVOLTINI DI VITELLO
Veal Rolls

1¼ pounds veal cutlet, sliced thin, Italian style	Butter
	White wine or broth as desired
¼ pound Mozzarella cheese	Salt
8 anchovies cut in strips	Pepper

Pound the cutlets thin and cut in 8 thin strips on which you place an oblong piece of Mozzarella and a strip of anchovy. Roll up the veal and tie with a thread. The veal rolls are browned in butter. Should the veal not be so young, the rolls can be generously moistened with white wine or broth and cooked a little longer. Season to taste with salt and pepper.

Both *scaloppine* and veal rolls go very well with a green salad. Serves 4.

SALTIMBOCCA
Little Veal Rolls (*Literally "Jump in the Mouth"*)

The author of a famous Florentine cookbook, Pellegrino Artusi, lists *saltimbocca* as a Roman specialty. The author of a Roman cookbook, Adolfo Giacquinto, ascribes the dish to the people of Brescia, but Ada Boni (who deserves a marble bust for her encyclopedic dissertations on Italian cookery in *Talismano della Felicita—The Talisman of Happiness*) is doubtful about *saltimbocca*'s claim to Roman citizenship; she points out, however, that it is seldom missing from Roman menus. Historians who have wasted so much paper and ink on wars should finally turn their attention to the much more delightful field of the history of cookery!

But no matter where *saltimbocca* originated, it is usually made of veal. It can also be made of *vitellone* (young beef or mutton), and this is just as good if cooked a long time.

ADA BONI

2 pounds veal cutlet, sliced very
  thin
8 thin slices smoked ham (or
  prosciutto)

8 fresh sage leaves (or ¼ teaspoon dried sage)
¼ cup butter
Water or dry white wine

The preparation is simple. Cut the veal into 8 strips (see page 105) and pound them as thin as possible. Place a slice of ham (cut to the same size) on each strip with half a sage leaf between the two layers. Roll the *saltimbocca*, fasten with toothpicks, and brown in butter. Pour a little water or wine over it, cover and cook till tender. The juice should be thick, but scant. Before serving, pour juice over the veal rolls. Serves 6.

SPEZZATINI DI VITELLO
Veal in Cubes

1 clove garlic, sliced
¼ cup olive oil
2 pounds shoulder or leg of veal,
  cut in cubes
1½ teaspoons salt
⅛ teaspoon pepper

½ teaspoon marjoram
4 bay leaves
4 sprigs parsley, chopped
½ cup dry white wine
6 fresh tomatoes or 3 tablespoons tomato paste

Brown garlic in olive oil and remove immediately, then put in the meat and sauté quickly. When it is beautifully brown, salt and pepper it, add marjoram, bay leaves, and parsley, and pour wine over it. When the wine has cooked down, add peeled and seeded tomatoes or 3 tablespoons of tomato paste. Now add water to cover and simmer, covered, till tender. This may take from 1½ to 2½ hours depending upon the age of the veal. Serves 4.

IL POLLO
Chicken

The old jungle bird, which even in the Bronze Age our ancestors counted among the companions and comforts of mankind, enjoys the highest respect in Rome.

The augurs studied chickens as they fed, and foretold the future—a method unsurpassed either by crystal balls or by astrological forecasts. Today *"Auguri!"* still means "Lots of luck!" and today, too, chickens still appear on the tables of the City on the Seven Hills on special occasions.

In the matter of chickens the Roman is not to be trifled with: his chickens must have been raised in the backyard and on open fields; then, brushed with oil, they are roasted on the fire of Vesta. Various experimenters who have raised chickens according to overseas methods (in modern chicken coops where, to the accompaniment of music, they lay eggs on the assembly line, and are fed according to strictly scientific principles on scraps from mills and stockyards) have been financially ruined. The Romans want their chickens *come Dio commanda,* "as God ordains."

POLLO ALLA DIAVOLA
Chicken alla Diavola

It is only natural that since the arrival of St. Peter, the Prince of the Apostles, in Rome, the devil has been an ever-present subject of conversation. Little good has been heard of him; depending upon the times, he was held responsible for the wording of the Koran, for the founding of Freemasonry, and for various political parties. The female members of the devil's family—as, for instance, in the North the devil's grandmother—are much more popular. The devil's wife is credited with inventing an original and delightful way of cooking young chickens. The result is so convincing that even the sternest judges of the *Sacra Rota Romana* have no objection to meeting the *pollo alla diavola* at their Sunday midday meal.

To prepare *pollo alla diavola* you need at least two charcoal stoves (or two burners). On one of them put several irons, not the modern type, but the heavy flatirons called sadirons which were used in olden times and which are perhaps still used in hell today.

1 young chicken (2 pounds)	Salt
2 teaspoons rosemary	Pepper
½ cup oil	Cognac

Pluck, singe, and clean the chicken, reserving the insides for a *sugo*. Place the chicken, breast down, on the table and with a sharp, heavy knife cut down the middle through the breastbone. The chicken can be cut into two pieces, but the original advice of the devil's wife is to cook it whole. If this counsel is followed, turn the chicken and lay it on the table like an open book, with the breastbone up. By strong pressure, or by a blow with the cleaver on the breastbone, flatten the chicken. Then let it marinate for a good half hour in rosemary and oil.

Salt and pepper it and put it on the grill (or in a skillet) and promptly lay one or two hot sadirons on it to press the chicken even flatter and at the same time to roast it from above. As soon as the irons begin to cool, replace them with hot irons. When you change irons you may take this opportunity to add a little oil to the chicken. In 20 minutes the chicken will have atoned for all its sins and is ready to be served. Serves 2 to 4.

On very special holidays you may remove the irons from the chicken in the pan in the last 5 minutes, and then pour a good cognac over it (or cognac and wine). Allow this cognac to evaporate. Anyone interested in learning this unusual method will find restaurants on the edge of the city, in particular on the old cemetery road on the Via Appia Antica, where this marvelous specialty is prepared.

POLLO ALLA CACCIATORA
Chicken Hunter's Style

The preparation is exactly the same as for *abbacchio alla cacciatora* (Lamb Hunter's Style—see page 98), except that white wine is used, never vinegar.

POLLO IN PADELLA
Chicken in the Pan

1 young chicken (2 to 3 pounds)	1 sprig rosemary
Raw ham	½ cup white wine
Olive oil	3 or 4 fresh tomatoes
Salt	Water or 4 sweet peppers
Pepper	Paprika
1 clove garlic	

The chicken, washed and cleaned, is cut in pieces and dried with a cloth. Cut raw ham in small rounds and fry in a pan with olive oil, then add the chicken pieces, turning them till they are handsomely brown. After that, salt and pepper them, and add garlic and rosemary to the pan. Immediately pour white wine over the chicken, and while it is evaporating, add 3 or 4 fine tomatoes, peeled and seeded. You may now choose between two procedures: you may add water, cover, and finish cooking the chicken until tender; or you may add peppers. The meaty yellow, green, or red peppers that come from near Naples are first laid on the grill over the fire, where they become soft, and the skin that covers them is easily removed. They are now done and may be added to the chicken just before serving. Chicken in the pan with peppers is a typical dish in summer. Sprinkle with paprika, if desired. Serves 4.

੪੪ PESCE
Fish

In the old days the sea came almost to the walls of Rome. Today, owing to the soil's being carried down and deposited by the Tiber around its former mouth, as previously mentioned, fish have to journey a long way before they land in Roman pots and pans. The result has been a marked progress in refrigeration. Fish from ports along the coast from Anzio to Civitavecchia reach the markets of the Campo di Fiori early every Friday morning, and their quantity and variety would put many an aquarium to shame.

Culinary science divides plants into herbs and weeds, fish into "big" and "little" (many people would say that human relations could be included in this latter category, for the "big" fish gobble up the "little" fish). The one inflexible rule is that little fish must be fried (see page 35) and big fish must be either boiled, broiled, or baked. The most delicious members of the big fish family are the *tonno,* or tuna fish; the shark-like *palombo;* the flat, flounder-like *sogliola* (sole), and the ray *arzilla.* We shall therefore give recipes for the most digestible way to eat the four big fish.

122

TONNO FRESCO AL POMODORO
Fresh Tuna Fish with Tomatoes

1½ pounds fresh tuna, in 4 slices	1 anchovy
Flour	½ cup white wine
Olive oil	1 tablespoon tomato paste
1 onion, sliced	1 bay leaf
2 cloves garlic	Salt
Parsley	Pepper

Fish and sauce in this case are prepared in separate pans. In the first pan sauté the lightly floured slices of tuna in a little oil till they are light brown, or until the fish flakes when tested with a fork.

In the second pan sauté onion and garlic in a little oil. Remove the garlic clove as soon as it begins to brown, and in its place put an anchovy rubbed with parsley. Over this mixture pour white wine, and when it is half evaporated, add tomato paste and bay leaf. Salt and pepper to taste.

Ten minutes before serving, pour the sauce over the sautéed fish, and let it cook in the sauce over low heat a few minutes longer. Serves 4.

PALOMBO CON PISELLI
Palombo with Peas

The *palombo* (a sort of dogfish) shows its relationship to the shark in its hard, scratchy skin. *Pescivendoli* (fishmongers) will remove this skin if you wish and cut the *palombo* into flat, boneless slices.

Olive oil	1½ pounds boneless *palombo*
1 onion, sliced	slices
2 sprigs parsley, chopped	Salt
3 cups shelled fresh peas	Pepper
3 tablespoons tomato paste	

In a deep pan with a little olive oil, brown lightly a finely sliced onion, with parsley. As soon as it begins to brown, add peas (they must be fresh, tender peas which will be done at the same time as the fish). Now cover the peas with water and add tomato paste to give the desired color. Roman peas are cooked in 10 minutes.

Five minutes before serving, add the *palombo* slices to the peas—they need no more time than this to be cooked through. Add salt and pepper at the last moment. Serves 4.

SOGLIOLA AL VINO BIANCO
Sole in White Wine

From each sole cut four flat fillets. This is an art which the housewife prefers to leave to the fishmonger. She contents herself with sautéing the fillets in oil or butter.

Fillets of sole (about 1½ pounds)	3 sprigs parsley
Flour	Butter
1 onion	½ cup light white wine
2 anchovies	Juice of ½ !emon

First dip the fillets in flour and lay them aside. Chop onion together with parsley and anchovies and sauté lightly in a little butter. When it begins to brown, add wine. The moment this comes to a boil, lay the slices of sole in the sauce, lower the heat, and cook a full 10 minutes longer. The juice of half a lemon and a tablespoon of butter add to the pleasure of this justly famous fillet. Serves 4.

ARZILLA
Ray

The meat of the *arzilla* has an excellent taste but is harder than that of the other fish mentioned.

2½ pounds ray	1 bay leaf
Oil	2 tablespoons butter
1 onion	2 tablespoons flour
⅛ teaspoon pepper	Juice of ½ lemon
4 sprigs parsley	2 teaspoons anchovy paste
⅛ teaspoon thyme	

Cut the ray in pieces and cook it in a little oil in a skillet over low heat (or over coals) with onion, pepper, parsley, thyme, and bay leaf, till tender. After half an hour, strain off the sauce and set it aside to cool. Now with equal amounts of flour and butter make a paste and pour the cooled fish broth over it. The onion that was cooked with the fish is chopped fine and, with parsley, the lemon juice, and anchovy paste, is added to the sauce. Cook sauce until slightly thickened. Return fish to sauce and reheat, or reheat fish and serve with sauce separately. Serves 4.

SARDE
Sardines

To those who live far from the sea a sardine is a little fish shut up with its fellow fish in a tin can, bathed in oil, and waiting for its devotees. To the Roman the *sarda* is a fresh, gleaming little fish, the best among the inexpensive variety, and is sold so cheaply only because cleaning and boning them take so much time.

Count on ¾ of a pound of sardines per person—especially as after removing heads and tails very little remains.

2 cups dry bread crumbs	1 clove garlic, minced
¼ cup olive oil	3 pounds fresh sardines
¾ teaspoon salt	Lemon juice
⅛ teaspoon pepper	

In a pan mix crumbs, oil, salt, pepper, and garlic in a little water and stir till they form a soft paste. Now in one or several individual oven-proof pans (or baking dishes), well rubbed with olive oil, lay out the cleaned sardines so that they seem to be swimming from the center to the edges. Spread the bread-crumb mixture over them and add a little olive oil. Put in an oven at 400°F. for about 15 minutes, or until fish is just done. The Roman housewife prefers to leave this task to the baker, who knows as much about *sarde* as about young lamb. Sprinkle the dish with lemon juice before serving. Serves 4.

We remind you that as sardines belong to the little fish, they may also be fried in hot oil, either plain or floured.

BACCALÀ IN UMIDO
Steamed Salt Cod

1½ pounds boned, soaked salt codfish	2 tablespoons tomato paste
1 onion, sliced	3 tablespoons raisins
3 tablespoons olive oil	3 tablespoons shelled pine nuts

Salt cod, indigenous to northern oceans, appears punctually every Friday in Rome's markets to compete with the fish that live in warmer waters. To be exact, it really appears Thursday evening. Housewives and *pizzicagnoli* (grocers) then begin to soak the cod, and the chick-peas that precede it, under running water (or turn on the faucet and let it trickle steadily over the fish). When the dried cod has soaked 16 hours or more, depending on the size of the fish, in fresh running water, most of the salt will have been removed and the fish can be ready for the table in 20 minutes.

Sauté onion lightly in oil. When it is lightly browned, add tomato paste and a little water and allow to cook gently. Then place the cod in the sauce, to which you have added a handful of raisins and pine nuts (*pignoli*) and simmer gently for 15 to 20 minutes. Serve on a warm platter. Serves 4.

BACCALÀ E PEPPERONI
Salt Cod and Sweet Red Peppers

1 salt codfish (about 2 pounds)	4 sweet red peppers
Flour	1 onion
Olive oil	4 fresh tomatoes

The cod, after being desalted, is boned, dipped in flour and oil, and fried in hot oil. Cut the peppers lengthwise and grill gently over a charcoal fire till soft (or place in oven or singe over gas flame), at which time you can easily remove the thin outer skin that covers them. Slice an onion and sauté in oil, add the tomatoes (in the amount of half the weight of the cod), and let simmer, stirring gently till half done, when you will add the sweet red peppers and continue simmering till done. Place the cod on a hot platter, pour the sauce over it, and serve. Serves 4.

CIRIOLE COI PISELLI
Tiber Eels with Peas

The Tiber eel, so an expert told me, should really be counted among the lampreys. Their soft skin and tender white meat places them among the special delicacies the Roman will not forgo when peas are ripe.

1½ pounds small eels	Pepper
1 onion, chopped	½ cup white wine
1 clove garlic, minced	1 tablespoon tomato paste
3 tablespoons olive oil	2 cups shelled fresh peas
Salt	Water

Cut the eels in 1½- to 2-inch pieces. Sauté onion and garlic lightly in hot oil in an earthen pot (if you have one that is top-of-the-stove-proof) or skillet. When the onions and garlic are just beginning to brown, quickly add the pieces of eel. As soon as they begin to color, salt and pepper them and pour white wine over them. Then add tomato paste and after that the peas. Cook for 10 minutes more and they will be done—if the peas really come from the Roman Campagna. Should the liquid evaporate too quickly, add a little water at the last minute. Serves 4.

ZUPPA DI PESCE
Fish Soup

To translate *zuppa* as "soup" is just as obvious as it is inexact. *Inzuppare* means "to soften by immersion, to soak." *Zuppa* can also be a sweet dish in which a cake is drenched in liquor. In the present case the *zuppa* will be poured over slices of bread.

Zuppa di pesce may be placed among the soups of the first course as well as under the *pietanze* (or main courses). It is a meal in itself. Romans eat it preferably in the evening in special fish restaurants on the Piazza Sant' Ignazio (they look like the ornate scenery for a Rossini opera) or somewhere between the Pantheon and the Corso. But the housewife who understands the art of buying can also compete with the famous fish cooks at home.

Like *pastasciutta, zuppa di pesce* is a favorite subject of conversation, though not everyone will approve of the others' variations. The question that is not yet settled is: who has the sole correct recipe?

Zuppa is prepared in different ways all along the coast. The Catanians insist upon adding raisins; in Sicily there must be plenty of fennel. The conservative Roman avoids both extremes. The truth is that the fish that swim along a flat coast are quite different from those found among rocks. Moreover fish taste different at different times of the year—and all of them have a different name every 30 to 40 kilometers. Sometimes a man who understands the local dialect can settle a quarrel by assuring the disputants that they are recommending the same fish under a different name.

Among the many possibilities, each man praises his own recipe and smiles condescendingly or maliciously at all the others. The Neapolitan praises San Gennaro (St. Januarius) and the *zuppa* as it is prepared in the famous restaurant Zi' Teresa (Aunt Teresa); the man from Bari considers St. Nicholas with his three gold balls more important, and fish soup with onions far better than any other. Each man prefers it as he tasted it for the first time in his childhood!

I learned the language and the *zuppa* of Rome from Sora Emma (Sora = Signora), the wife of the porter in the ancient house in which I had the good fortune to live. Even before World War II it was not so easy to find a bed between the Piazza Navona and the Tiber in the *ponte* district, where stand the house of the Rossini family, the birthplace of Pope Pius XII, and ancient military towers like the Tor Millina . . . and so I praise the *zuppa* of the good woman who had seen more than half a century of Roman history herself. To be more accurate, she saw what went on between the Piazza Navona and the Tiber, for she clung strictly to the tradition that a respectable matron never leaves the confines of her own little district. And why should she, when every district has a charcoal dealer, a wine merchant, a drugstore? When she was a little girl Sora Emma had once been on St. Peter's Square— and that completely covered her travel needs. On Fridays, however, she never failed to go to the Campo di Fiori to buy fish, although on that ten-minute walk she had to cross the

Corso, the boundary line of her kingdom. I considered it a special privilege to be allowed to accompany her and carry her bag.

Our way led from the Via del Corallo past the Palazzo Braschi, the Fascist Party secretariat. At one corner of that palace stood the old, ruined statue popularly called Pasquino, to which it had formerly been customary for Romans to attach rhymes, jokes, and puns mildly criticizing the government. As Fascism did not tolerate any form of criticism, even a mild or humorous remark, Pasquino had been silent for almost twenty years.

"*Se ne andranno*—someday they'll scram," Sora Emma remarked casually and nodded toward the stately Palazzo Braschi. As at that time—the beginning of 1939—there were countless foreign ministries throughout Europe that still did not know this, I assume that her *zuppa* recipe is based on equally sound information. For anyone who wanted to learn about the fish of the Mediterranean, the flora and fauna of central Italy, and at the same time the speech of Rome, one could not think of a more instructive walk.

For three hundred years the Campo di Fiori has been the most colorful market in the world. Until the year 1600, however, things were not so pleasant here. On the corner opposite the French Embassy (today the Cancelleria) they used to burn at the stake those people who strove for sainthood in their own fashion. In the holy year 1600 there was no carnival, and to give the people a little pleasure the authorities decided to bring the philosopher Giordano Bruno, who had taught that there were other worlds beside our solar system, out of the prison on the Via Tor di Nona, where he had already sat for six years, and burn him. The French ambassador pro- tested—not against the decision, but because the smoke and the stench of the burning monk had blown into his windows. The authorities were courteous and considerately moved the stake to another location. Ever since then the Campo di Fiori has been a vegetable and fish market.

The statue of Giordano Bruno looks toward the opposite side of the market where there are flowers and herbs, and turns its back on the fish. Sora Emma and I, on the other hand, went straight to the corner where strange names were being called aloud. *Cefalo! Merluzzo! Arigusta! Capitonno!* I assumed they were the names of the devil in one of the cooler circles of Dante's Hell. But Sora Emma said: "Those are the fish we want."

Even she didn't know all the sea monsters by name, but she pointed to a truly devilish fish:

"That is the *pesce San Pietro,* St. Peter fish. It tastes awfully good and it hasn't many bones. We'll buy it. Do you see the fingermarks on the right and on the left? That's where the Apostle grabbed him and made those marks!"

St. Peter must have been a strong man! In the church of Santa Francesca on the Forum they show the marks of his knees. He had knelt on the stones of the Forum and prayed while the devil carried Simon, the magician, through the air to divert the people's attention from Peter's preaching. The prayer was successful, the devil flew off, the wicked magician fell to the ground—and let anyone who doubts this thrust his fists into the impressions made by the saint's knees.

"We want big fish and little fish," Sora Emma declared, "and we want squid." So we bought small squid (*calamaretti*), white mussels (*telline*), black mussels (*cozze*), and a goodly number of crabs.

"That gives the sauce a good taste," Sora Emma said. "The bigger, the better," she added. "Great big crabs, the *aragoste* (the spiny lobster) are the best. Their tail has white meat; the taste comes through."

We also bought a large quantity of garlic bulbs, a lot of parsley, and were given a little fire-red pepper for good measure (because Sora Emma demanded it energetically and complained that the garlic was too dear). "*Ci vuole*," said Sora Emma, "we need it. Now we have everything. There's enough pepper at home."

In front of the charcoal stove, surrounded by earthen pots of all sizes, I waited for further orders.

"Slice the garlic in small slices, young man," commanded Sora Emma (this was before World War II).

"Won't it be too much?" I asked in my inexperience.

"Garlic never hurt anybody," she replied severely. She was busy cutting off the heads of the little fish which her cat (or was it a little gray tiger?) immediately disposed of.

"*Certi signori*—certain people," she announced, "make a broth out of the heads and bones and pour it over the *zuppa*. I give them to my cat." Whereupon she poured a generous half glass of oil into a deep earthenware pot, set it over the coals, and fanned the fire till the sparks flew. "Now in with the garlic!"

I shook all the slices into the pot, where they began to dance.

"*Certi signori* let the garlic brown and then take it out. I leave it in."

I merely nodded.

"The *calamaretti* are nice and young, but they take the longest in the *zuppa*. They go in first."

With that she tossed the squid into the hot oil. After they

had crackled for a while, she added pieces of the larger fish, which I thought were parts of shark, rays, and flounders. When they had all taken on a good color, Sora Emma put fresh coals under the pot and when they were fanned to a bright glow the fish were returned to their natural element—salt water—in which they obviously felt better.

"Come on, cut the bread," Sora Emma ordered and pressed several old loaves into my hand—the longish loaves whose name you won't find in any dictionary, but which the baker calls *sfilatini*. I sliced them obediently. Meanwhile Sora Emma put the mussels in a deep pot with water to cover.

"*Certi signori* make such a fuss—*tante storie*—because there's always a little sand left in the mussels. Why shouldn't there be when you find them in sand? I just wash them. If there's a little sand left, it'll sink to the bottom."

Now the mussels went into the *zuppa,* and last of all the crabs and the crab-like, armored *aragoste,* the lobsters. Enough water was then added to permit them to move around freely. "Fish, squid, mussels, crabs," Sora Emma repeated the litany. "*E guai si qualcosa manca!* And woe if anything is missing!"

The *zuppa* began to smell truly inviting. One or two tomatoes added greatly to the color, which had been rather gray. Sora Emma then tossed in ground pepper and whole peppercorns and at the last the extra-sharp red pepper she had been given.

"*Certi signori,*" she said again, "put in either pepper or hot red peppers. I put in both. Pepper never hurt anybody."

I had been convinced for some time that these *signori* had no conception of the right way to make *zuppa di pesce* and would do better not to try.

Now Sora Emma (who quite rightly had no faith in my skill) lit a second charcoal stove, and set a large, flat pan containing oil on top of it.

"For the bread," she said.

"Can't you toast the bread on the same fire?" I asked naïvely, and was immediately sorry I had spoken.

"The *zuppa* will be poured hot over the toasted slices, not cooled."

I did not venture to ask any more. Besides, the *zuppa* was already done. The dry *sfilatini* slices eagerly drank up the oil that I had thought was too much. Piping hot and brown, the bread slices were then laid in the deep, warmed soup plates. They hissed and the soup steamed as it was poured over them. I noticed that the bread was perfectly toasted, for it had preserved its consistency. Now one after the other the principal ingredients were spooned out: fish, crabs, mussels, and squid that had shared the Mediterranean now shared the same plate.

Since that day I have spooned many a fish into the *zuppa di pesce* and have read many books about it. I now know that some soups are colored yellow with saffron and have bay leaves, fennel, and orange peel added. . . . I know fish soups whose genius somehow belongs to the followers of Neptune, like the *cacciucco* of the Tuscan coast in which wine is first poured over the fish in oil; the *bouillabaisse* of Marseilles, which, in addition to garlic, also contains onions and leeks. . . . If I were rich and had a yacht, I would visit all the little harbors along the western Mediterranean and sample the *zuppa*

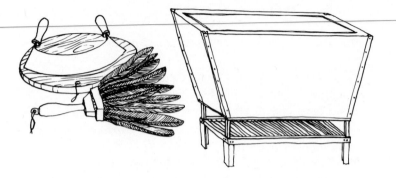

on the Balearic Islands, in Corsica, and in Sardinia . . . but I myself would never dare to prepare it other than the way I learned it from Sora Emma. I would not like to be classed among *certi signori.*

ZUPPA DI PESCE I
Fish Soup (Plain) for One Person

Olive oil
Garlic
1/5 pound of squid
Generous ½ pound of large and
    small fish
A handful of mussels

Several crabs and if possible a
    piece of lobster tail
Tomato paste
Pepper
Red pepper
Parsley
Slices of white bread

In a deep kettle in which a generous amount of oil has boiled, brown a garlic clove which you have cut in half. Put in the squid first, then add the big fish, then the little fish, and finally mussels and crabs, and cover all with water. A little tomato paste, a little pepper, and one sharp red pepper complete the *zuppa,* which does not need more than 20 minutes to cook.

Sprinkle generously with chopped parsley when the seafood is done.

Pour the hot *zuppa* over slices of white bread (preferably Italian or French bread which has been dipped in olive oil and toasted). Those who wish to save on oil, or to keep their figures, may toast the bread over the fire (or in a toaster).

ZUPPA DI PESCE II
Fish Soup (for Special Occasions)

The quantity of fish per person is the same as in the preceding recipe, but here preference is given to the boneless big fish like tuna, *palombo* (dogfish) and ray.

1 lobster	3 sprigs parsley
Several different kinds of seafood as in preceding recipe	1 or 2 anchovies
	1 piece sharp whole red pepper
1 onion	Dry red wine
1 carrot	Olive oil
1 stalk celery	Tomatoes
Several garlic cloves	White bread

Divide the lobster into tail and breast pieces, split breast in half. Loosen the fillets from the *sogliola* (sole) and bone the small fish carefully. Heads and bones are tossed into a separate pot with one onion, one carrot, and celery, covered with water, and cooked for 20 minutes. Strain the broth through a piece of cheesecloth. Crush together a few garlic cloves, parsley, 1 or 2 anchovies, and a little piece of sharp red pepper, and soften in dry red wine.

When you have finished these preparations, set a copper or other heavy kettle (or an earthenware crock) on the stove and heat olive oil in it. When it is hot, add the wine with herbs and let it simmer. Peel and seed several tomatoes and add to the mixture in the kettle. Add the fish broth.

Now put in the squid first (as Sora Emma observed, they are somewhat harder) and cook slowly in the fish broth till tender. After about a quarter of an hour add the lobster, and 10 minutes later the other pieces of fish and the carefully scrubbed and prepared mussels and juice. (The mussels should first be allowed to open in a very small quantity of oil over high heat. Then pour water over them, remove the meat from the shell and beards and strain the juice through a cloth; by this method, to be sure, you deprive the guest of the pleasure of opening the mussels himself.)

The finished *zuppa* is then poured over slices of white bread which have been toasted or fried in oil.

ZUPPA DI PESCE III
Fish Soup (Peasant Style)

In the days when Fiumicino had not yet become the site of Rome's international airport but was still a picturesque fishing village, it boasted a number of small *osterie* that served a simple and very good fish soup made of the cheapest fish— without any lobster tails. Use approximately the proportions in the two preceding recipes per person.

Oil	Parsley
Tomatoes	Various fish
1 sharp red pepper	Sea water
Garlic cloves	White bread

In a pot in which water is boiling put oil, peeled and seeded tomatoes, a whole red pepper, several garlic cloves, and parsley. Clean the fish, salt them with the sea water, and cook quickly in this savory brew.

This simple soup, like its complicated relatives, is poured over toasted bread slices.

LUMACHE
Snails

The church of St. John Lateran (San Giovanni in La-terano) is known as the "Mother and Head of all churches." It has always been the first official act of any Pope to take possession of the noble Basilica. Even in our day the con-secration of the Pope is followed by a solemn procession from St. Peter's to the Lateran, the only difference being that the Holy Father no longer travels by one horse's power, but in his multi-horsepower Rolls-Royce.

At other times the church is seldom visited. For the Ro-mans it lies out of the way—far behind the Colosseum, on the outer city walls. For strangers, it has little interest, par-ticularly since in the last century it was renovated with very poor taste. Even the heads of the Apostles Peter and Paul, which are still preserved over the altar, have lost much of their charm for tourists, who may now visit an apostle's grave below St. Peter's. In Holy Week, when chorales from Palestrina and his contemporaries are sung, the church is still visited by music-loving sight-seers.

However, the great attraction that draws vast crowds to the church of the beloved apostle are the snails which, on the day of the solstice—San Giovanni—are served in all the *osterie* and *trattorie* in the Lateran district, exactly as they were in the days when men were more pious.

The circle of vineyards around the city supplies not only

wine but also edible snails, the special dish eaten on St. John's Day. And though few of my readers will have the opportunity to practice preparing edible snails, we shall nevertheless give the method which at the end of their lives brings them again into contact with the wine of their native habitat.

The snails spend their last day in a huge basket where they are given a last breakfast of grape leaves and bread moistened and squeezed dry. On the feast day itself they are put into salted vinegar water to which they react by giving out foam. This same treatment is repeated until they stop foaming. They are then washed off in clear water several times, at which point the situation becomes serious—they are tossed into a kettle, with water to cover, under which a hot fire is burning. While the water is still lukewarm, they stick out their feelers in delight—but only to come completely out of their shells as the heat increases. In 10 minutes they are cooked. They then wait in cold water for their sauce, which is extremely simple to make.

Sauté 2 sliced cloves of garlic in 2 tablespoons of olive oil till brown, then remove them from the oil. In the same oil crush several anchovies with a wooden spoon. Add 6 fresh tomatoes, seeded and peeled, salt, a lot of pepper, 1 whole red pepper, and a mint leaf to complete the harmony of this dish. Cook over low heat, add the snails, and let them simmer gently for half an hour. (For 4 to 6 persons prepare 4 pounds of live land snails and sauce as given.)

Then we are ready—processions, fireworks, music—everything adds to the festive mood, but when all is said and done it is the snails that give the feast of San Giovanni its true character. And if the sauce is too sharp you may cool your throat with one or two glasses (or more) of wine from the Castelli Romani.

᷇᷇ VERDURE
Vegetables

In Rome vegetables do not play the modest role compared to meat that they do in many places. A plate of green peas is considered a complete *pietanza*—second course. Tuna fish or ham may appear as a modest accompaniment to the peas.

In the North, vegetables are boiled or steamed, then thickened with sauce or served with butter. Not so in Rome, where

the general practice is first to sauté them in butter or oil and then to pour water over them. This is possible because the vegetables of the Roman Campagna are especially tender and can be cooked quickly. Artichokes, peas, and broccoli are the particular pride of the Latium region, which was once the heart of the Roman Empire and today still rules supreme as the producer of the finest artichokes, peas, and broccoli.

CARCIOFI ALLA ROMANA
Artichokes Roman Style

Stuffing: For each large artichoke	Salt
use	Pepper
½ cup softened bread	Artichokes
2 anchovies	1 lemon
2 sprigs parsley, chopped	2 tablespoons oil
1 peppermint leaf	

First prepare a stuffing by mixing bread with water and squeezing out most of the moisture. Mix with anchovies, parsley, peppermint leaf, and salt and pepper to taste. Next, cut off the hard tips of the leaves of the artichokes and cut the stems, leaving about 1¼ inches. Rub the whole artichokes with a lemon and place them in lightly salted lemon water. While you are heating oil in an earthen or metal pot, take the artichokes, one by one, out of the water, spread them on the table, pressing them so that the leaves open, and put the stuffing between the leaves, then press leaves back into place. Lay the artichokes with the stem up in the hot oil. Immediately pour in enough water to half cover the artichokes. Now put the lid on the pot and let them cook till done, which with real Roman artichokes takes no more than 20 minutes.

CARCIOFI ALLA GIUDIA
Artichokes Jewish Style

The German historian, Ferdinand Gregorovius, who wrote the history of Rome and was made an honorary citizen of the city, has published an excellent chapter on the history of the Ghetto. He can be criticized on only two points: in the last sentence he discarded his role as historian for the role of prophet; and he forgot the most famous discovery that was ever made between the Palace of the Cenci and the old Forum Holitorium (vegetable market).

He prophesied that by this time in our tolerant and humane century the history of sufferings in the Ghetto would have finally come to an end. His failure was in not leaving us a recipe for preparing artichokes. This is strange, as even the great sonnet poet Giacomo Belli, who was well known to Gregorovius, states emphatically:

> *Non c'e principe o re christiano che sia*
> *che nun magni carciofi alla giudia*

which freely translated means:

> Princes and kings, heathens and Christians
> All eat artichokes Jewish style.

Young artichokes	Pepper
1 lemon	Oil
Salt	Water

To prepare artichokes this way, you must use only young artichokes that are almost round and have green leaves. Cut them so that the stem is only about 1 to 1½ inches long. Slice off the top layer of the artichoke tops, tear off the hard outer leaves, and trim the points of the leaves. Unless it is stainless, be sure to wash the knife you have used promptly and thoroughly in lemon juice, then place the artichokes immediately in lemon water. Never put them in an iron pan, as contact with this metal darkens artichokes. An enamel or porcelain pot is better, but if possible always cook them in a seasoned earthen pot.

Then, seizing the artichokes by the stems, flatten them on the table so that the leaves open far enough to permit you to salt and pepper them inside. Now put them in the pot, into which you have poured a generous amount of lukewarm oil. Place them with the stems up and fan the charcoal fire to such flaming heat that the oil begins to bubble briskly. Now press the artichokes so firmly against the bottom of the pot that the leaves—which have now become hard, crisp, and light brown—open quickly like a chrysanthemum.

Sprinkle cold water over the hot oil. The steam that rises helps to open the artichokes and soften them a little—in case they are not quite young or the oil has been used too often and is "tired." The artichokes must remain crisp and look like flowers—and must be eaten immediately. Allow about 4 small young artichokes per person.

PISELLI AL PROSCIUTTO
Peas with Ham

1 onion, chopped	⅛ teaspoon pepper
3 tablespoons oil or butter	Water or broth
3 cups shelled fresh peas	Raw ham
¼ teaspoon salt	

Sauté a finely chopped onion in oil or butter until lightly browned. Then add the fresh young peas, salt and pepper, and pour water or broth over them. Cook quickly over high heat. Fresh peas from the Rome region will be done in 10 minutes. Meanwhile use this time to cut into small pieces several slices

of raw ham from Parma or Norcia (*prosciutto di montagna*, raw ham from the mountains, is a special favorite) and add them to the peas a minute or two before serving. When you salt the peas, remember that the ham itself is fairly salty. Serves 4.

BROCCOLI ALL'AGRO
Pungent Broccoli

Broccoli	Salt
Olive oil	Pepper
Lemon juice (or vinegar)	

Broccoli is the characteristic vegetable of autumn. The green rosettes are cut off, leaving on about an inch of the stalk, and cooked in a little water till tender. When done, drain and add oil, lemon juice (or vinegar), salt and pepper. *Broccoli all'agro* may be served either hot or cold.

FAGIOLI AL TONNO
Beans and Tuna Fish

The most suitable beans for *fagioli al tonno* are the *fagioli della Regina,* the Queen's beans—brownish-white beans which are picked before their pods are quite dry. Boil them, drain, and mix them with canned tuna, oil, and a few raw onion rings and serve. Use salt and pepper sparingly. In Rome grocers keep tuna in large cans and sell it by weight, which is much cheaper than buying small cans.

POMODORI RIPIENI
Stuffed Tomatoes

Tomatoes are available all year round and tomatoes filled with rice can be found in every *rosticceria*. They may be eaten before, after, or instead of a larger meal.

6 large tomatoes	⅓ cup chopped parsley
Uncooked rice	1 clove garlic, minced
Salt	6 tablespoons olive oil
Pepper	2 basil leaves, chopped

Take large round tomatoes and cut off ½ inch of the upper portion so that you can put it on again as a cover. Remove the juicy pulp and reserve it in a deep dish. Then half fill the tomato shells with rice which you have picked over care-

fully but not washed. Salt and pepper them, sprinkle them with finely chopped parsley and a little garlic, and pour 1 tablespoon olive oil into each. Purée tomato pulp and strain. Mix with basil and pour into each tomato, and the "covers" you have cut off are now put on again. Bake the tomatoes slowly in a moderate oven, 350°F., until the rice is tender but not too soft. Serves 6.

FUNGHI AL TEGAME
Sautéed Mushrooms

2 tablespoons anchovy paste	1 clove garlic
¼ cup sweet butter	Salt
1½ pounds mushrooms	Pepper
3 tablespoons olive oil	A mint leaf, if desired
4 large tomatoes	

Though the idea of combining mushrooms with anchovy paste may seem odd, the result is worth a trial.

In a saucepan mix 2 tablespoons of anchovy paste with butter and allow it to cook down and soften. (Or preferably make your own paste from anchovies mixed with sweet butter. To do this remove any bones from anchovies, pound anchovies in a mortar, and mix well with sweet butter.) Wash, wipe, and slice mushrooms, then sauté in oil, stirring over medium heat for 10-12 minutes until the water in the mushrooms is greatly reduced. Add tomatoes peeled, seeded, and drained, and garlic (remove garlic as soon as cooked). Add anchovy-butter mixture and heat. Salt and pepper complete this dish, to which in Rome they like also to add a mint leaf. Serves 4.

PEPERONI
Sweet Peppers

The peppers may be green, red, or yellow, but they must be sweet, not sharp and hot. Cook the sweet peppers till soft on a grill over a charcoal fire (or place in a hot oven, 425°F., or singe over gas flame), so that the thin outer skin may be easily removed.

Open the peppers, remove and discard seeds, cut in thin strips lengthwise, salt lightly, pour oil over them, and serve either hot or cold. (They may be fried in oil if desired.) Allow 2 large peppers per person.

✌✌ DOLCI, FRUTTA
Desserts, Fruit

Why think about cakes and pastries when one has just eaten heartily of *pastasciutta*, fish, and roast beef? And when every season of the year brings us the choicest fruit?

Spring brings wild strawberries from the woods around Lake Nemi. They are so fragrant and fresh it seems almost a sin to season them with sugar and red wine as so many people do, especially as Crème Chantilly (whipped cream) is always ready to accompany them! Scarcely is the strawberry season over than our eyes turn toward the hill town of Arezzo, not because it has the finest frescoes of Piero della Francesca, but because of the incomparable cherries from this region. Preserved in alcohol, they last a long time—at least until they have fulfilled their destiny at wedding banquets and baptismal feasts. Toward the end of June they are replaced by melons, which are more often served with ham as an hors d'oeuvre than with sugar for dessert. The melons are followed by figs, which make an ideal breakfast with a piece of *pizza*—a flat bread brushed with oil. Early autumn brings peaches from Castel Gandolfo, and they reign supreme till winter comes with its oranges and mandarins from Sicily. In

between there are also grapes from the vineyards of the Castelli and Vesuvius, and the muscatel grapes of Pantelleria. There are nuts from Sorrento and for hot summer days ice cold *cocomeri* (watermelons) . . . for cold winter nights, roasted chestnuts from the woods on Monte Amiata. And all this wealth of fruit takes little trouble to prepare and gives much pleasure. In any case, it is an excellent reason for spending the whole year in Rome, once you are there.

On very special occasions pastries are served between *pietanze* and *frutta*. They are seldom made at home, which would not be easy on a charcoal stove (although you could put heat on the cover of the pot and bake the contents that way). It is preferable to buy the *dolci* from the pastry shop.

Turin is the home of expert pastry cooks. The city lies so close to France that the French *pâté à chou* and *éclairs* have had no difficulty in finding their way to it over the route once marked out by Hannibal. When the Kings of Savoy, "by the grace of God and the will of the nation," moved to Rome, the pastry cooks came with them. Their activities proved to be more useful and they themselves more stable than the rulers. The ruler on the Quirinal became an Ethiopian Emperor and vanished from sight; the *pâté à chou* (puff paste), on the other hand, filled with superlative *zabaglione* (made with Marsala, egg, sugar, and cream) has endured.

When you are invited to the home of especially old friends for midday dinner, you can offer to bring the pastry with you. That will give your host a welcome opportunity to open a bottle of Salento or Marsala from southern Italy, or a Lacrima Christi from Vesuvius, so that the time until black coffee is served may be pleasantly employed.

LA CROSTATA
The Cake

Crustula, the Romans called the sweet cake, and from *crustula* to *crostata* is only a step . . . a mere two thousand years! Take 2¼ cups of sifted all-purpose flour, 1¼ cups sugar, ⅔ cup of butter, and 2 egg yolks, and out of this quickly make a dough. Add a little cold water if necessary. Let it rest for half an hour. Refrigerate if too soft to handle easily. Then divide it in two equal parts. One half is rolled out on a floured board to fit a 9-inch pie pan. The other half is rolled out to be used to make a lattice work on the cover.

Traditionally, cherry jam is spread in the crust, but our century is not so fond of cherries, and other jams of the same color, even currant jam, are used in its place. Spread 2 cups of jam on the crust. (Sometimes the *crostata* appears as an apple cake. To make an apple *crostata* put 4 cups sliced pitted apples into crust. Sprinkle with 3 tablespoons sugar and 1 tablespoon dark rum. Spread with ⅔ cup jam or jelly.) Over the jam lay strips of dough in the shape of lattice work, the last piece being used to form the edge of the *crostata.* Bake at 375°F. for 40 to 45 minutes or until crust is golden brown. Serves 6.

BIGNÈ DI S. GIUSEPPE
St. Joseph Fritters

Philologists say that the word *bignè,* which does not appear in most Italian dictionaries, derives from the French *beignet.* But according to Larousse the French word comes from the Celtic *bigne.* As the Gauls invaded Rome in 387 B.C. (to be sure, Livy forgets to tell us whether, besides *"Vae victis!*" Brennus said anything about the preparation of baked desserts), Rome seems to be using the original word.

Bignè (at home and on the street) are baked on the 19th of March, St. Joseph's Day, and are eaten in his honor. They then disappear from the menu again for a year.

The characteristic of these fritters is that the dough rises in the frying pan (in oil or butter) and forms a hollow ball. On other occasions this round or oval shape would be filled with cream; but on St. Joseph's Day they are left hollow, sprinkled with vanilla sugar, and eaten hot.

1 cup water	¼ teaspoon salt
½ cup of butter	1 tablespoon sugar
1¼ cups sifted all-purpose flour	1 teaspoon grated lemon rind
3 eggs	Oil for frying

Butter and water are brought to a boil in a saucepan; at that moment remove the pan from the heat, toss in flour, and stir rapidly. Set the pan back on the heat again and stir vigorously till the dough forms a ball, and does not stick to pan. Remove from the heat and allow to cool. When it is cool, stir in 3 whole eggs one at a time—each one only after the one before it is thoroughly incorporated. Keep stirring vigorously until the dough forms a few bubbles, then add salt, sugar and grated lemon rind. When all these ingredients have been well worked together, set the dough aside and let it rest for several hours. Heat oil for deep fat frying. Small pieces of this dough— the size of a cherry—swell in the hot oil to the size of an egg. The quantities given will make easily 70 or 80 *bignè*. As the finished *bignè* are likely to collapse the moment they cool, they must be eaten promptly before you make a second batch.

FAVE DEI MORTI
Beans of the Dead

This is the melancholy name of a cake that is eaten on All Souls' Day.

1 cup sugar	½ teaspoon cinnamon
⅓ cup butter	1 egg, beaten
1 cup finely ground unblanched almonds	¼ cup sifted all-purpose flour
	1 tablespoon grated lemon rind

Combine sugar, butter, and almonds. This marzipan is then worked together with the cinnamon, egg, flour, and rind.

Form this mixture into pieces the size and shape of a large lima bean. Put them on a well-buttered baking sheet, and bake in a moderate oven 350°F. In 15 or 20 minutes they are golden brown and done, even when they look soft. Cool 5 minutes before removing from pan with a spatula. The longer they stand the harder they become and the better they taste. Makes about 50 "beans."

FRITELLE DI RISO
Rice Fritters

Fritters made of cooked rice can be fried in the pan in hot oil and need no oven.

Rice
Oil
Vanilla sugar or sugar and
  cinnamon

Cook the rice at first very briefly in five times the amount of water and then let it simmer on the back of the stove 2 hours longer until it is completely boiled to a thick mass.

This mass must now rest several hours, if possible a whole night. It is then ready to be spooned, a little at a time, into boiling hot oil and fried to a crisp brown. Before serving, sprinkle the fritters with vanilla sugar or with sugar and cinnamon.

PAN DI SPAGNA
Spanish Bread

Pan di Spagna is a fluffy, light cake that may be covered with various creams and marmalades and drenched with any sweet liqueur. Housewives usually buy it at a pastry shop and add the last touch (the liqueur) themselves. The batter, which is at home everywhere under different names, is easy to make:

6 eggs, separated	1¼ cups sifted cake flour
1½ cups sugar	¼ teaspoon salt

Beat 6 egg yolks till lemon colored, with sugar. Carefully fold in cake flour. Whip 6 egg whites and ¼ teaspoon salt until stiff but not dry, and carefully fold into first mixture. Pour into 2 buttered and floured 8-inch deep layer pans or any other pans of about this capacity. Bake in moderate oven, 375°F., about 40 minutes. Turn onto cake racks and cool.

ZUPPA INGLESE
Tipsy Cake

Without a doubt the most popular way of serving *pan di Spagna* is *zuppa inglese*. Why Spanish bread, soaked with rum from Jamaica and Alchermes from Florence, should be called English is one of the mysteries of cookery which perhaps not even the archangels understand. In Rome it has long been known that there are such mysteries and that one should not try to solve them.

Zuppa inglese consists of two or more layers of *pan di Spagna* bound together with a cream filling, drenched first with rum and then with Alchermes, and topped with whipped cream. Each layer may be split in half if only two are baked. The cream filling is made as follows:

4 egg yolks, beaten	Dash salt
¼ cup sugar	2½ cups rich milk, scalded
1 teaspoon grated lemon rind	1 tablespoon butter
¾ teaspoon vanilla extract	

Mix yolks, sugar, rind, vanilla, and salt together in a heavy saucepan. Slowly add hot milk, beating constantly with whisk or rotary beater. Cook over low heat, stirring constantly, until mixture boils. Cook just long enough to make a thin custard which will slightly coat a metal spoon. Stir in butter. Let cool. Stir occasionally to discourage formation of a skin.

Alchermes is a fragrant red liqueur. Historians who write the story of Western liqueurs mention Florence as its home. There in 1482, the physician Michele Savonarola, uncle of the unfortunate Girolamo, wrote a book on the beneficial effect of alcohol. In those days alcohol was not made out of potatoes or grain, but distilled from the noble wines of Crete and Malvasier. It was discovered that alcohol would prevent meat from spoiling, and the idea of prolonging man's life by copiously imbibing *aqua vitae* (the water of life) seemed to be the obvious conclusion. Even today alcohol is known to have a beneficial effect on old people: a glass of brandy makes them feel rejuvenated. Michele Savonarola already knew an *aqua vitae composita,* a brandy in which spices were dissolved or herbs distilled or a liqueur that turned yellow with saffron. (The Carthusian monks, whose rule gives them time to meditate, soon discovered the healthful action of yellow and green liqueurs—Chartreuse.) The Medici, owners of the leading banking house in Europe, who could indulge themselves in many luxuries, are said to have ordered from Cosimo Ruggieri an elixir that prolonged life. He called it Alchermes. The alcohol contained cinnamon, nutmeg shells, cardamom, and cloves, and was colored bright red with the newly discovered cochineal. The Popes from the House of Medici, Leo and Clement VII, brought the Alchermes to Rome, where, to be sure, it is seldom drunk today, but is indispensable in *zuppa inglese*.

Zuppa inglese is generally served in round cups without a handle. Pastry and layers of cream alternate, whipped cream being added on top as a crowning touch.

MARITOZZI
Raisin Breakfast Rolls

Maritozzi are just as good at breakfast as they are in the afternoon with coffee, and are especially good *con la panna,* with whipped cream.

1 package active dry yeast	2 eggs, beaten
1 cup lukewarm water	¼ cup oil
4 cups sifted all-purpose flour	½ cup sugar
¾ teaspoon salt	⅔ cup seedless raisins

Mix yeast with ½ cup of lukewarm water in mixing bowl. Stir in 1 cup of flour and mix well. Turn onto floured board and knead a few minutes. Form into a ball and return dough to bowl. Cover with a damp cloth and let stand in warm, but not hot, place until doubled in bulk. Put remaining flour in a mound on board. Make a depression in the center and fill with remaining ½ cup lukewarm water, salt, eggs, and oil. Mix into flour with fork, then with hands. Knead several minutes and work in the yeast dough and sugar. Knead until very smooth, then add raisins and knead again. Shape into egg-sized balls and put at least 4 inches apart on greased baking sheet. Let stand in warm place until doubled in bulk. Bake in moderate oven, 375°F., for about 15 minutes. Makes about 24 rolls.

To make them look especially decorative, they are brushed with sugar syrup and put in the oven for exactly 1 minute more.

ST. HONORÉ
St. Honoré Cake

The French claim St. Honoré and his cake. "He was Bishop of Arles and died there in 429," they say. Romans insist, on the contrary, that he was, according to the holy Bishop Hilarius, an ancient Roman from a family that had also produced consuls. "A virtuous life need not be a sad one," he used to say, and even as abbot he took care that a merry mood reigned in his cloister. He is therefore the right choice for patron saint for a cake the mere sight of which makes one's mouth water. Whereas the other saints are mentioned on only one day in the year, Romans give thanks to St. Honoré every Sunday.

The protectorate of this delightful saint is, however, not undisputed. Another St. Honoré, patron saint of France's bakers, also has a claim to being considered the saint to whom this cake is dedicated. He lived from the year 554 to 600; his miracles were written down in the twelfth century and depicted in the Amiens Cathedral. King Childbert tried to have his relics moved from Amiens to Paris, but a divine power held them fast. St. Honoré gave the bones of the three holy martyrs Fuscianus, Victorius, and Gentianus, which had been shown to the hermit Lupicianus by an angel, an honorable burial. Is that perhaps the reason for the three different colored creams in the cake? However, the borderline between hagiography and pastry-baking has not yet been sufficiently explored and we shall not venture to solve the problem here.

The cake itself is simple and decorative: a thin, round layer of baked puff paste to which a crown of *bignè* is attached with caramelized sugar, but this time the *bignè* are filled. The crown of puffs is divided into three sections, one of which is covered with puffs filled with plain whipped cream, the second with puffs filled with the yellow cream (see *Zuppa inglese,* page 154), and the third with puffs containing a brown cream filling made of whipped cream mixed with grated chocolate.

✌ ✌ VINO
Wine

All the dishes of Roman cookery, from the most modest *pastasciutta* with garlic, oil, and peppers—*aglio, olio, peperoncini*—down to the juiciest roast, have one thing in common: they appear on the table accompanied by wine. "Rather nothing but bread and onions, if only it is in Rome," says the Roman citizen emphatically and modestly, when told about better living conditions abroad. He will be satisfied with a *sfilatino*, an onion, and a few drops of oil—but his glass of wine he must have.

The water in Rome is excellent. In the old part of the city the fountains, *le fontanelle*, flow day and night. The water system, the oldest parts of which were laid by the censor Appius Claudius Caecus, are still in use. From Trevi, from the hill country, the clearest, purest, coolest water flows to the city. At the Forum the fountain of the nymph Egeria still flows. Anyone walking about the city and feeling sudden thirst has not long to search. He soon finds a fountain and need only know how to close the pipe with his finger and catch the stream of water that rushes upward. He will learn to drink, too, out of the hollow of his hand.

But when you sit at a table, that is a different matter. Water that has been standing does not taste so good as flowing water. That is when you reach for the wine. . . .

But which wine shall you choose? The stranger who has not yet taken to heart Metternich's fundamental dictum that "Italy is a geographical concept" will make mistakes: he will ask for a Chianti or a Lacrima Christi in Rome!

The simplest rule is for the wandering gastronome to choose the local specialties wherever he may be. Through ignorance (also because the teaching of geography in schools so criminally neglects the subject of menus) he will sin heavily. The man who would ridicule a Chinese looking for eel soup in Vienna or Austrian *Backhendl* (roast chicken) in Hamburg is capable of asking for *lasagna col ragù* in Rome as if he were strolling under the arcades in Bologna.

But the man in Rome who orders the wines of the Castelli Romani (Roman Castles) with his meals will not make a mistake. They are definitely made to drink "by the dome of St. Peter's."

The *castelli* surround Rome in a wide half circle from the south. No two of them are alike. Some are ancient: Albano is the Mother of Rome; Rocca di Papa was built in the Middle Ages. Some were lordly estates like Marino, while others were originally fortresses. Castel Gandolfo is today (or, more correctly, is again) the papal summer palace; but all the *castelli* are surrounded by vineyards. Cloisters and Cardinals' villas, week-end houses, villas built by moving-picture beauties of *Cinecittà* for their husbands who needed a rest—all of them overlook vineyards.

The chain of *castelli* that have seen so many battles, and even in the last World War heard the guns of Anzio booming, now protect the capital only against thirst. The most important wine regions whose gardens, peach orchards and vineyards adjoin one another are Frascati, Marino, Grottaferrata, Albano, Genzano, and Velletri. Between dry white Frascati and the heavy, red, sweet Cesanese of Grottaferrata there are countless nuances, but a description of those wines is not so thrilling as tasting them on the spot.

In the same group belong the wines from vineyards in the immediate neighborhood, like the especially fragrant, sweet red wine of Subiaco, the dry red of Olevano, that little town beloved of artists before they became abstract painters, and the light red Cecubo of Sperlonga, *Vinum Caecubum,* the wine of which Horace sang.

Small *osterie* generally carry only three or four kinds: a dry white wine; a sweet; a *sulla vena,* a semi-sweet; and a red wine. To get a more knowledgeable picture one must stroll around the city.

At noon many families have their liter of wine from the

Castelli brought from the nearest *trattoria* (if they have not brought a little cask home from their Sunday outing by car).

Bottle or cask . . . what a special problem that is no one has made so clear to me as Heinrich Hase, the friendly little Saxon, whom the god of war and his own love of peace had driven to Rome. He lived not far from me, and we used to meet at noon when we went out to get our wine, and, like many foreigners, to pick up our mail at the main post office in San Silvestro. (The Romans call the post office "San Silvestro"— mistakenly, of course. St. Silvester is the patron saint of the nearby church in which one of the many heads of St. John the Baptist is preserved.) As we came to know each other better, Hase told me his secret.

"I've discovered a system for saving on stamps," he said.

"You don't write often?" I asked naïvely.

"No, no. A system based on a psychological foundation."

I looked surprised.

"Yes, yes! Postal clerks are poorly paid. They don't like to work. I don't like to work either, do you?"

"Of course not."

Hase was obviously delighted to find this resemblance between us.

"Look at this letter! It weighs a little over an ounce. I'm sending it to Leipzig. Registered. Costs a fortune!"

"Two hundred lire?"

"More. I've already been to the first window. They weighed it—two hundred and seventy-two lire! I can get it cheaper."

I doubted that.

"Postal clerks are tired," Hase now repeated and leaned toward me. "Look here!" He pulled a bunch of stamps out of his pocket: three twenties, seven fives, two twelves, a big commemorative stamp at forty, one at twenty, seven at one. . . . It would have been something for a collector!

"Three more fives of the oldest issue—but they're still good—seven threes . . . now, how much is that?"

"Heaven only knows!"

"That's my system. Two hundred and twenty-two! Do you want to count it up? Wait a moment: the twelves are fastened to the fives . . . you won't get far by multiplying them. The forty you can see plainly. I've never had a postal clerk count up the stamps. That's fifty saved right there!" He seemed to have grown several inches taller. "Hase's postal savings system!" he exclaimed proudly.

I was away from Rome for a short time, but after my return I met him again. I had noticed that he did not come to fetch his wine any more.

"Have you given up drinking?" I asked him. "I don't see you at Peppino's nowadays."

"I'm not such a fool," he replied. "That is, I drink my two glasses of Marino at every meal—but buy it from Peppino? No, siree! I have a savings system."

The one with postage stamps had been ingenious . . . but how does it work with Peppino, I thought to myself, though I didn't dare to ask his secret. However, because we were such good friends, he finally confided in me.

"My wife has an uncle out in Marino. We go to see him now and then on Sundays. And there you can get the same wine in hundred-liter casks. The uncle delivers fruit in the city, brings the cask with him, and we roll it into the dining room. Would you like one too?"

I lived on the fifth floor in an artist's studio and the last flight was as steep as a chicken ladder. The thought of climbing up those five flights with a hundred-liter cask did not attract me. Moreover my bar balance on that day would cover no more than one liter.

"And do you know what it costs? I'll tell you! Just exactly half! To the penny, exactly the half!"

There was no doubt about it—Hase was a genius at saving. I was therefore all the more surprised shortly after that to see him with his one-liter bottle at Peppino's.

"Herr Hase!" I called to him. "You're paying too much. What's happened? What about your system!"

"*Non va,*" was his somewhat embarrassed reply. "Won't work."

"But doesn't it cost only half by the cask?"

Hase did not answer immediately. Swinging the bottle to and fro, he hesitated, then said finally: "Yes, I counted it up again. It costs exactly half. But . . . but . . . d'you know: we drink much more than double the amount!"

☜☜ PIZZA

LA PIZZA NAPOLETANA
Neapolitan Pizza

"*Andiamo mangiar una pizza!* Let's go and eat a pizza."
. . . These words mark the beginning of the evening program
of many families, lovers, and countless visitors to Rome.
There is always a good reason for eating a pizza: in winter
because the weather is cold, and the sight of the fire crackling
and glowing on the charcoal stove delights and warms you;
in summer because most pizzerie set their tables and chairs
in the open and you can breathe in the cool evening air.
You may decide to go out for a pizza because it is a cheap
supper or because you have already eaten supper and still
have room left for it. Or simply because you want something
good to eat or because you need an excuse for drinking, a
causa bibendi.

The pizza will not be ready—it is made fresh for everyone.
And the diner who cannot wait patiently had better order
something else. Meantime, while waiting for the pizza to be

166

cooked, let us learn something more about this unusual dish. Why is it called *pizza napoletana?* Does it really come from Naples? There are Romans who dispute this. "Cooks give their inventions strange names," they say. "Does *Zuppa inglese* come from England?" Or, "They call this *pizza napoletana* to distinguish it from the plain pizza." This plain pizza (flat bread) as it comes piping hot out of the oven, brushed with a very little oil, is a favorite of Romans, especially when it is accompanied by fresh, green figs.

When you have eaten pizza in Rome as well as in Naples, you are inclined to agree with the Roman. The Neapolitans leave a broad, dry crust and generally sprinkle too much marjoram on it, and the only cheering part of the meal is the view over the Gulf of Naples, which is particularly fine from the heights of the Vomero.

A Neapolitan gastronome whom I questioned did not deny that the pizza in Rome is better. "But why is that?" he immediately went on. "Do you think the Romans invented it? Do they want to take the pizza away from us too? I'll tell you why you get better pizza in Rome. They've stolen our best cooks from us . . . that is, when they don't go straight to New York," he added with a sigh.

That same round, flat bread is depicted on the frescoes at Pompeii. The black buffaloes, from whose milk Mozzarella cheese is made, graze in the country around Naples. But we shall carefully refrain—especially as the argument can become quite violent—from discussing such a ticklish subject as whether one should drink the wine of Capri or the wines of the Castelli with it. In such cases it is well to come out with a sentence that is sure not to be disputed, such as, for instance: "Lucky the man who lived in Rome after the discovery of pizza and before the invention of the Vespa."

The most expensive restaurants in the world allow you to pay for the pleasure of watching them make pancakes and cook ducks. In the *pizzeria* you may have such pleasure much more cheaply. The chef works with his back to the oven and the ingredients for the pizza spread out before him. He has no secrets. With the precision of a pianist he allows us to see his finger technique. Everyone is free to study his method and to imitate him.

Here on his left stands the bowl containing the finished bread dough. It has been well worked by hand and is now rolled flat with the rolling pin—by dint of some exertion. You must pull off a piece that is just the right size and roll it out in a round, flat shape. What the right size is depends on whether the pizza is intended for one, two, or four persons. Beside the bowl for the dough lies the Mozzarella. This moist cheese with its covering lies in whey. It must never be dry. To eat it raw would be a crime; it is tough, hard, and apparently tasteless, but heat turns it liquid and yellowish and brings out its incomparable quality.

Next come whole raw tomatoes that have been peeled and seeded and to which several basil leaves have been added. You may also use canned tomatoes, for whatever you may say about Neapolitans, to insert basil into whole tomatoes is an art which only they understand.

Generous supplies of salt and freshly ground pepper are also at hand, but we advise the greatest caution with salt, for the anchovies, boned, split, and laid in oil, come from a salty element.

For a special pizza, mushrooms (fresh or dried—in the latter case softened in water) are prepared—and of course there must be plenty of oil. Before the pizza goes into the oven, it must be brushed carefully with oil. And here one must avoid extremes, neither too much nor too little: in *mediis tutissimus ibis*—safety lies only in moderation.

When the waiter—with the seriousness and emphasis of a ship's captain giving his helmsman an order—shouts *"Una*

pizza," the virtuoso performance begins: the dough is rolled out in a circle and covered to the edges with cubes of Mozzarella; four or five tomatoes are decoratively laid on it; the anchovies are spread out with the correct gesture; pepper is sprinkled over it and oil poured out—whereupon a second expert comes on the scene: the fire-tender.

The bake oven is hot, through the open door comes a gust of warm air, but the slow-working heat would never produce a proper pizza! The moment the pizza is in the oven the fire-tender must pull a piece of glowing coal under it and then fling just the right amount of shavings on the fire—enough to make it blaze up furiously and give out so many calories that Mozzarella, tomatoes, oil, and anchovies melt together into a soft, smooth, fragrant mass—without letting the crust become dry or even brown. At exactly the right moment the pizza must be taken out of the oven and the waiter, this time as winged as the fleet-footed Achilles, must set it in front of the guest before the fragrant waves of cheese and oil have entirely subsided.

It is a real loss to German literature that there was no pizza when Goethe took his evening strolls with his Faustina. Only a poet of his rank could have done justice in verse to the preparation of pizza, a task impossible to accomplish in prose.

It is a great temptation to make this work of art at home and with ordinary means. For instance: instead of bread dough, one could take leftover cake dough; instead of Mozzarella, any sort of cheese that can be diced or cubed; instead of anchovies, sardines; instead of fresh tomatoes, canned tomatoes—and instead of olive oil one could use vegetable or peanut oil. All you have to do then is put the pizza in the oven. . . . However—the friendly reader who follows the above method is respectfully requested to reread the story of the farmer's wife in the castle—and this time a little more attentively!

IL CALZONE
Ham and Cheese Pizza

A more rewarding task is to make the kind of pizza filled with ham and cheese that is known as *calzone* (trousers). This pizza too tastes best when it is hot and is straight out of the oven. It will make several servings.

1 package active dry yeast	¼ cup butter, softened
¼ cup lukewarm water	6 ounces Mozzarella, cubed
2 cups milk	½ cup chopped cooked ham
1 tablespoon oil	Salt
About 3 cups all-purpose flour	Pepper

Add yeast to water and let stand 5 minutes. Heat the milk to lukewarm, add oil and yeast, and stir constantly till thoroughly mixed. Then add flour and work it quickly into dough which can be handled. Put the dough on the top of a floured table and knead it a few minutes. Sprinkle with more flour. Cover it with a cloth and let it rise. In half an hour test the dough by pressing it with your finger. If the dough immediately springs back, it is ready and may be rolled out.

Now spread butter (or half butter, half lard) over the

dough, fold the dough over once, and work butter and dough vigorously together. When the butter is evenly distributed through the dough, divide dough into thirds, roll out each to ¼ inch thickness, and transfer to greased baking sheets. Cover one half of each round of dough with the Mozzarella cheese and the ham. Sprinkle with salt and pepper and fold the other half over the half you have covered. Bake the *calzone* about 25 minutes in a hot oven, 400°F. It is customary to serve it on a cloth.

A NOTE ABOUT THE RECIPES

Olive oil is often specified in this book and it should be used. However there are times when just "oil" is listed. In such cases, any cooking oil may be used: corn, peanut, cottonseed, safflower, or an oil blended of two or more oils. Some blended oils contain olive oil.

When a recipe calls for fat, any solid fat may be used: hydrogenated, lard, or rendered pork or beef fat which solidifies at room temperature.

When fat or oil for frying appears in the ingredient list, no amount is specified. The circumference and depth of the utensils used for frying vary to such a degree that it is impossible to specify the exact measure.

While old Roman households always had (and some still have) seasoned ceramic or earthenware pots made for cooking over the fires then used, generally speaking it is unsafe to surface cook on our modern gas and electric units in just any present-day utensil, other than those of metal. We do have some Pyroceram and glass such as Pyrex flame-proof ware which is excellent for such use. A few flame-proof ceramic casseroles, skillets and Dutch ovens are imported from Europe, but one must follow the directions of the manufacturers of both the utensil and the range when cooking over direct heat. A utensil may be heat-proof (meaning oven-proof) yet *not* flame-proof. All glassware sold to be used for surface cooking is marked *flame-proof*. However, any dish suggested in this book may be made in modern stainless steel, enameled ironware, seasoned black ironware, heavy aluminum or any other utensil of good weight and quality. Thin, cheap cookware is never a good choice for lengthy cooking where scorching is likely to take place.

These recipes have been tested with conventional all-purpose flour and cake flour. When it is sifted before measuring, sifted flour is specified. It is not recommended that the instant-type flours be used. Do not use any type of self-rising flour in these recipes.

GLOSSARY

Travel guides and dictionaries that are usually so reliable fail the visitor to Rome at the very point where he needs them most—on the threshold of restaurants. Even books that guide you conscientiously all through Dante's Inferno break down lamentably between *antipasto* and *dolci* (appetizers and desserts).

The following list of two hundred words, though far from complete, will take the reader safely through the menu in his *trattoria*, even in those cases where the Roman dialect differs from other Italian.

A

abbacchio, baby lamb
acciughe, anchovies
affumicato, smoked
aglio, garlic
agnello, lamb
agnolotti, filled pasta cases (ravioli)
agro, sour (*all'agro:* with oil and lemon)
al, allo, alla, on, in, at, in the style of
alici, anchovies
amatriciana, woman from Amatrice (town in the Abruzzi)
animelle, sweetbreads
antipasto, appetizers
arancia, orange

174

arrosto, roast
arzilla, ray (fish)
asciutto, dry

B

baccalà, dried salt cod
basilico, basil (herb)
bignè, fritter (sometimes filled)
bistecca, beefsteak
braciolina, cutlet
broccoletti, turnip greens (a green vegetable)
broccolo, broccoli, variety of cauliflower
brodettato, cooked in broth (boiled)
brodo, broth, soup
bucatini, short, cylinder-shaped dough (noodles)
budino, pudding
burro, butter
burro fuso, melted butter

C

cacciatora, alla, hunter's style
cacio, cheese
calamai, calamari, calamaretti, squid
calzone, a pastry filled with ham and cheese
Campo di Fiori, Rome's vegetable market
cappelletti, garnishing for soup (hat-shaped)
carciofo, artichoke
carne, meat
carota, carrot
Castelli Romani, the castles around Rome (wine region)
cavolfiore, cauliflower
ceci, chick peas
cena, supper

cerase (ciliege), cherries
cervello, brain
ciliegia, cherry
cipolla, onion
ciriola, Tiber eel (also a long roll)
cocomero, watermelon
colazione, breakfast
con, col, colla, with
conserva, preserve (also canned food)
coppiette, meat balls, chopped meat
coratella, heart, lungs, liver (of lamb)
coscetto, leg, shank
cotechino, sausage
cozze, black mussels
crostata, fancy cake, tart

D

di, dello, della, of, from, of the
diavola, devil (feminine), the devil's wife
dolce, sweet (*il dolce*, dessert; *i dolci*, sweet dishes)
dorato, dipped in egg yoke and baked

F

fagioli, beans
fagioli della Regina, Queen-beans, or freshly picked beans
    that are still soft
fava, large bean (broad bean)
fava dolce (dei morti), an almond pastry (on All Souls' Day)
fegatelli, liver slices
fegato, liver
ferri, the grill (grilled or roasted on the grill: *ai ferri*)
fettuccine, noodles
filetto, the fillet

fiore, flower

fornello, cook stove (for coal)

fragola, strawberry

fragolina, wild strawberry (found in the woods)

Frascati, a famous wine-producing town in the Castelli Romani

fresco, fresh

friggitore, man who grills meat or cooks it on a spit

frittella, baked sweet, fritter

fritto, anything fried

frutta, fruit

funghi porcini, edible Boletus and other edible mushrooms (*Agaricus campestris*)

fungo, mushroom

G

gallina, hen

giovedì, Thursday (Thursday potato noodles: *Giovedì gnocchi*)

gnocchi, potato dumplings, potato noodles

guanciale, bacon

I

indivia, endive (salad)
insalata (verde), a green salad
involtini, little rolls

L

legumi, pod vegetables
lenticchie, lentils
limone, lemon
lombello (lumbello), loin (of the pig)
lumaca, snail

M

maccheroni, macaroni (tube-shaped dough)
maiale, pig
manzo, beef
maritozzi, little rolls of dough made with yeast
mascarpone, soft cream cheese
mela, apple
melanzana, eggplant, aubergine
minestra, the first course, soup
mortadella, large sausage
Mozzarella, a cheese made, in Italy, of buffalo's milk; in America of cow's milk

N

noce, the nut
noce moscata, nutmeg
Norcia, town in the Apennines, center of pork butchery and smoked meats, home of the black truffle

O

olio, olive oil
olive, olives

P

padella, frying pan
pagliata, small intestine (ox gut)
pagnotta, round loaf of bread
pan di Spagna, cake (literally Spanish bread)
pane, bread
panini, rolls
panna, cream, whipped cream
parmigiano, Parmesan cheese
pasta, dough
pastasciutta, noodles (macaroni, spaghetti, etc.)
pastina, noodles for soup
patata, potato (fried potatoes: *patatine fritte*)
pecorino, sharp sheep's cheese
pepe, pepper
peperoncino, (sharp) pepper pod, sharp red pepper
peperone, Cayenne pepper
pera, pear
pesca, pesche, peach, peaches
pesce, fish
pescivendolo, fishmonger
petto, breast
piatto, plate, dish (food)
piccioni, doves, pigeons
pietanza, the second course
piselli, peas
pizza, flat bread
pizza napoletana, bread dough with cheese and tomatoes (hot)
polenta, cornmeal

pollo, chicken, fowl
polpetta, chopped meat, croquette
pomodoro, tomato
porchetta, roast pork
porco, pig
poverella, poor woman
pranzo, lunch (midday meal, early dinner)
prezzemolo, parsley
prosciutto, ham (raw)
provolone, a cheese

R

ravioli, pockets or envelopes of dough with a filling
regaglie (rigaglie), heart, liver, gizzard of chicken
ricotta, cheese made from milk curds
rigatoni, short, tube-shaped noodles
ripieno, filled, the filling, the stuffing
riso, rice
rosmarino, rosemary
rosticceria, rôtisserie (roasting on the spit)

S

sabato, Saturday (on Saturday there is tripe: *sabato trippa*)
salsa, sauce
salsiccia, sausage
saltimbocca, little meat rolls
salvia, sage
sarde, sardine
scaloppina, cutlet
semolino, grits of wheat (semolina)
seppia, squid
sfilatino, longish roll of bread
soffritto, fat with herbs

sortaceti, mixed pickles
spaghetti, long, thin strips of dough (noodles)
spezzatino, meat cut in pieces
spiedo, grill or spit
spuntino, light meal, snack, refreshment
stracciatella, egg-ribbon soup
stravecchio, very old (for example, Parmesan cheese)
stufatino, boiled or stewed meat
sugo, sauce, juice, a dip
sul, sullo, sulla, on the, upon the
supplì, rice dumplings
sventola, fan

T

tacchino, turkey
tartufo, truffle
tegame, the pan (fried in the pan or pan-broiled: *al tegame*)
telline, small mussels
testa, head
timballo, in a timbale or pudding mold
tonno, tuna
tortellini, round garnishings for soup
trippa, tripe (calf's or cow's stomach)
tritato, chopped

U

uccelletto, little bird
umido, wet (braised meat: *l'umido*)
uovo, egg
uve, grapes

V

vaccinara, dairymaid
vecchio, old
vena, sulla, semi-sweet (wine)
vino, wine
vitello, calf or veal
vongole, small mussels

Z

zabaione, Marsala wine with sugar and egg
zampone, pig's foot
zucca, pumpkin
zuppa inglese, cake soaked with liqueur

SUGGESTED ROMAN RESTAURANTS

Abruzzi (classic restaurant), via Frattina 192
Angelino (typical Roman *trattoria*), piazza Margana 37
L'Antico Falcono, via Trionfale
Cacciani, Frascati (about 12 miles from Rome)
Capriccio (distinguished classic restaurant), via Liguria 38
Capricciosa (restaurant-pizzeria), largo dei Lombardi 8
Casina della Rosa, gardens of the Villa Borghese
La Cisterna (typical Roman *trattoria*), via della Cisterna 13
Galeassi (modern restaurant), piazza Santa Maria in Trastevere 3
Hostaria dell' Orso (distinguished restaurant), via Monte Brianzo 93

Hostaria Giggi Fazi (typical Roman restaurant), via Lucullo
22
Meo Patacca (typical restaurant), piazza dei Mercanti 30
Il Pescatore, via dell'Acqua acetosa
Re degli Amici (Artists' restaurant), via della Croce 33/b
Romolo (local Roman *trattoria*), via di Porta Settimiana 8
Tavèrna Flavia, via Flavia 9
Tre Scalini, Piazza Navona 30

Restaurants Noted for Special Dishes
(Pizza is equally good everywhere)

Alfredo alla Scrofa, via della Scrofa 104   FETTUCCINE
Alfredo all'Augusteo, piazza Augusto Imperatore   FET-
TUCCINE
Il Buco (Tuscan *trattoria*), via Sant'Ignazio 9   BEEFSTEAK
S. Callisto, via Appia Antica   CHICKEN ROMAN STYLE
Caminetto (classic restaurant), viale dei Parioli 89   LAMB
Checco er Carettiere (typical *trattoria* of the quarter), via
Benedetta 13   SPAGHETTI
Corsetti (typical restaurant), piazza San Cosimato 28   SEA-
FOOD
Ernesto (Roman-style cooking), via del Vaccaro 1   SEAFOOD
Passetto (modern elegant restaurant), via Zanardelli 14
ARTICHOKES ROMAN STYLE
Piperno (Roman *trattoria*), via Monte Cenci 9   ARTICHOKES
JEWISH STYLE
Valle—La Biblioteca (characteristic tavern), largo Teatro
Valle 7   CHICKEN ROMAN STYLE
Vincenzo (local *trattoria*), via della Lungaretta 173   FRITTI,
ZUPPE DI PESCE

TABLE OF APPROXIMATE
WEIGHTS AND MEASURES

The flour used in these measurements is all-purpose flour unless otherwise designated. The "one glass of wine" mentioned in the recipes is a generous 4 ounces (½ cup).

FLOUR WEIGHT (all-purpose)

Metric	British	American
2 grams	½₂ ounce	1 teaspoon
6 grams	¼ ounce	1 tablespoon
100 grams	3½ ounces	1 cup
454 grams	16 ounces (1 pound)	4½ cups
1000 grams (1 kilogram)	2.2 pounds	10 cups

CAKE, PASTRY FLOUR

25 grams	2¾ ounces	1 cup
100 grams	3½ ounces	1¼ cups
454 grams	16 ounces (1 pound)	5⅜ cups
1000 grams (1 kilogram)	2.2 pounds	12 cups

BUTTER

15 grams	½ ounce	1 tablespoon
112 grams	4 ounces	½ cup
450 grams	1 pound	2 cups

Metric	British	American

FISH

| 500 grams | 1 pound (generous) | 1 pound (generous) |

MEAT

| 500 grams | 1 pound (generous) | 1 pound (generous) |

RICE

| 240 grams | 8 ounces | 1 cup |

SUGAR (granulated)

5 grams	⅛ ounce	1 teaspoon
15 grams	½ ounce	1 tablespoon
60 grams	2 ounces	¼ cup
240 grams	8 ounces	1 cup

APPROXIMATE EQUIVALENTS
FOR
LIQUID MEASURES

1 liter	1¾ pints	4¼ cups or 1 quart 2 ounces
½ liter (1 demiliter)	¾ pint (generous)	2 cups (generous) or 1 pint (generous)
⅒ liter (1 deciliter)	3–4 ounces	½ cup (scant) or ¼ pint (scant)

INDEX

187

5 Days in Rome

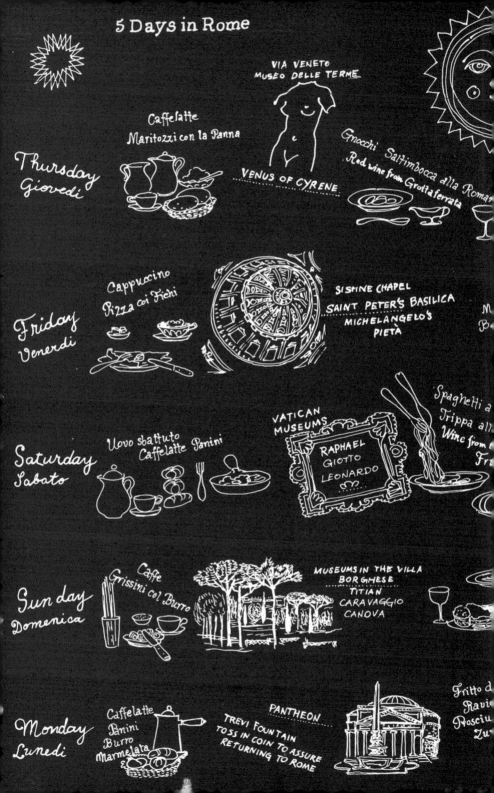

VIA VENETO
MUSEO DELLE TERME

Caffelatte
Maritozzi con la Panna

VENUS OF CYRENE

Gnocchi Saltimbocca alla Roma
Red wine from Grottaferrata

Thursday
Giovedì

Cappuccino
Pizza coi Fichi

SISTINE CHAPEL
SAINT PETER'S BASILICA
MICHELANGELO'S
PIETÀ

M
B

Friday
Venerdì

VATICAN
MUSEUMS

Uovo sbattuto
Caffelatte Panini

RAPHAEL
GIOTTO
LEONARDO

Spaghetti a
Trippa all
Wine from
Fr

Saturday
Sabato

Caffe
Grissini col Burro

MUSEUMS IN THE VILLA
BORGHESE
TITIAN
CARAVAGGIO
CANOVA

Sunday
Domenica

Caffelatte
Panini
Burro
Marmelata

PANTHEON
TREVI FOUNTAIN
TOSS IN COIN TO ASSURE
RETURNING TO ROME

Fritto d
Ravic
Rosciu
Zu

Monday
Lunedì